McKenzie Scott's 15 New Rules for Job Hunting Success

The Art of Marketing Yourself Into The Right New Job or Career

The McKenzie Scott Client Handbook

Bob Gerberg

McKenzie Scott
PERSONAL MARKETING SERVICES

McKenzie Scott, 7979 East Tufts Avenue Parkway, Suite 1400
Denver, CO 80237 • 800-320-1277 • Fax 303-357-3923

With 30 million resumes in circulation, don't get trapped by these common misconceptions.

"I think my resume is really good."

"I can always get a job with my network."

"All I need to do is answer ads."

"I'm very marketable... I'll get a job quickly."

"If I get the interview... I'll get the job."

McKenzie Scott's 15 New Rules For Job Hunting Success, 2nd edition Copyright © 2005, 2006 by C.A.N. Inc. All rights reserved. No part of this book may be used or reproduced in any manner whatsoever, except in the case of brief quotations in articles and reviews. Publication date March 15, 2006. Library of Congress Catalog Card Number 2005938073. ISBN 0-9745114-5-5 (hard cover), ISBN 0-9745114-6-3 (soft cover). Published by McKenzie Scott Press, 7979 East Tufts Avenue Parkway, Suite 1400, Denver, CO 80237 • 800-320-1277 • Fax 303-357-3923.

Printed and bound in China.

Everyone who looks for a job should follow these job hunting rules.

If you look for a new job, you can expect some real challenges in today's market. Finding the right job is no easy matter.

McKenzie Scott is America's leading supplier of job changing resources. Based on our experience with tens of thousands of job campaigns, if you follow these 15 rules you will have an immense competitive advantage. They've been proven under tough market conditions.

This book is provided to our clients as part of the initial stage of our service to them. It covers all the essential job hunting knowledge that we believe you should be familiar with.

For those who are not our clients, this book will acquaint you with our philosophy. Regardless of your interest in our firm, if you are looking for a new position, the principles of professional job search which it covers can prove invaluable.

Major appreciation is given for the creative support, desktop publishing and design contributions of this book by Angie Hunckler of McKenzie Scott. Significant editorial and content contributions were made by McKenzie Scott partners Dan McAneny and Drue Pollan.

About the author

Bob Gerberg is among America's foremost authorities on every aspect of professional job hunting. More than 7 million copies of books and programs he has created are in circulation.

His ideas have been instrumental in helping millions of people throughout the world who have looked for new positions. Over more than 20 years he has authored dozens of books and audio cassettes.

These include publications such as *The Professional Job Hunter's Guide, The Professional Job Changing System, An Easier Way to Change Jobs, Sixty Great Letters Which Won New Jobs, $100,000 and Above—The New Realities of Executive Job Hunting* and many others.

He has also written numerous articles and published complete job hunting programs. These include *The Career Advancement Series*... a package of 28 small booklets on vital job hunting subjects. He has also authored programs that have consisted of six to sixteen audio cassettes... supplemented by eight specialty publications. These include *TAPIT, The Personal Marketing Program, The Executive Job Changing System* and others.

Over the years, hundreds of thousands of these programs have been used in outplacement and job hunting assistance programs by institutions ranging from the U.S. Marine Corps and the CIA through major universities, associations and numerous Fortune 1000 corporations.

Initially with GE, after his service as a U.S. Air Force officer, Bob's early career was with major food companies, including positions as a VP Marketing Services and Assistant to the Chairman of a Fortune 500 firm.

Active in the career field for over two decades, he licensed a system for executive job search to independent career firms worldwide… from 1987 to 1997.

With the emergence of the Internet, he formulated the architecture for their new approach to finding positions in the 21st century. McKenzie Scott is America's leading provider of job changing resources. The firm has assisted tens of thousands of professionals and executives in achieving their career goals.

Mr. Gerberg has a B.A. from Colgate University, a year of studies sponsored by the United States Air Force, an M.B.A. from the University of Pittsburgh and advanced executive studies at MIT, sponsored by PepsiCo. A resident of New York and New Jersey for most of his career, he and his wife Joan now reside in Denver, Colorado.

About this McKenzie Scott client handbook

Obviously, you've recognized that this book offers *15 New Rules For Job Hunting Success*. But, the important thing for you to keep in mind is that McKenzie Scott uses them—not because they are the firm's—but because they work… optimally. And, that's why you will want to follow them. This book shares the important fundamentals the firm has learned, in an easy-to-read and straightforward way.

Thanks to the worldwide reach of the Internet, 250,000 people will read extensive portions of this book online. In addition to copies that are sold, 250,000 complimentary copies will be shipped worldwide. This includes books to executive recruiters, employment professionals, HR executives and others. In 2005, this will have been the most widely read publication on professional and executive job hunting.

THE 15 NEW RULES FOR JOB HUNTING SUCCESS

Some thoughts from the author

For over 20 years I've been researching the job market and analyzing how professionals can find new jobs more easily. During this time, I've seen the employment markets go through some remarkable changes.

Since most of us rarely look for a job, we never really develop any expertise at marketing ourselves. What's more, not even our top schools educate us on the job market challenges we are likely to face. Did you know that every year, for the past 20 years, whether in good economies or bad, the time it takes to find a good new position—*has grown longer*?

Of course, 20 years ago, the job market wasn't nearly so complex. When someone looked for a job, their Sunday paper was jammed with classified ads. And, if that wasn't enough, major national papers like *The Wall Street Journal, The New York Times, The Chicago Tribune,* and *The Los Angeles Times* could be used to uncover more positions.

Answering ads was always competitive, and if that didn't work, you could visit a few recruiters or do some networking. Some might also have tried direct mail to CEOs. Other than that all you needed was a resume with a historical format... and some good references.

What happened to make job hunting so complicated? From time to time, the U.S. Labor Department has put out some depressing statistics... all relating to how long it takes for people to find jobs. In 2004, with 132 million employed, the government worried because 9 million Americans were out of work. However, *The New York Times* claimed that 6 million more were not included in the statistics... because they had given up.

Here's what's made things so competitive. For some time we've been in the midst of a communications revolution.

With the ability to use PCs, faxes and emails, people now distribute many millions of resumes—*each week*! They didn't do that previously. The growth of the Internet alone has changed forever the magnitude of resumes in circulation.

Why are there so many people in the market? Because of financial pressures, employers routinely go through staff reductions when sales decline. This has led to sharply declining employee loyalty. The concept of long term employment has disappeared from the American landscape.

Now, instead of looking for a job every 7 to 10 years... people change jobs on an average of once every 3.5 years. This alone has doubled historical levels of job market competition. Another factor is that people are living and working longer.

Further complications stem from the emergence of job boards. Many people now leave their resumes posted on-line—even after they accept new positions. So, in today's job market, we have both active and passive job seekers. One major job board claims that 47 million resumes are in their database—which they sell to employers as a recruiting tool.

The bottom line is that we now have a level of competition that was unimaginable just a decade or two ago. At least ***30 million resumes are circulating at any moment in time... while the jobs available are only a fraction of that number.***

To succeed in a job search today, you must first have an understanding of the new job market and how it works. This book will do that for you.

You will also need to get connected to the openings and leads you require. Using advanced technology is the only way to bring this information to your fingertips.

Today, people also face an additional challenge. To be effective, you need to communicate through multiple resumes, letters, emails and conversations. Marketing yourself is not so simple. Your need for clear messages across all forms of job hunting communications is critical. You must get your credentials into play on a large scale, and cut through the clutter that exists because of millions of other resumes, letters and emails.

It will also be important for you to succeed in "competitive interviewing situations." Even after you get the interviews you want... you need to recognize that there will often be 5 to 10 other candidates under consideration.

These considerations are why most people, if they depend on old job hunting methods, have an exceedingly small chance of connecting with a really good job. Given this climate, one of the first things I recommend is that you decide where your career fits with respect to other priorities in your life.

Chances are, to get the right job, you need to make an investment in yourself. Today, more and more people are equipping themselves with the resources and support they require... and spending some money to gain a competitive advantage. For many employed people, and especially two-income families, there are not enough hours in the day for them to properly market themselves. Increasingly, they turn to others for the resources and marketing support they need.

Of course, the thought of investing in yourself, and specifically a need to spend some of your savings on your search, may represent a cultural change for you. If this is the case, you should start by reviewing where you and your family spend discretionary funds. Even people with the same gross incomes will vary substantially. For example:

Some of us spend $2,000 to $5,000 on flat screen TVs; others spend $1,500 to $8,000 on private schools; many people take expensive vacations to Disney World or Vail, Aspen, Las Vegas, New York or Europe and so on; millions invest $80,000 to $160,000 for an MBA; and we also routinely acquire such things as mountain bikes, PCs, designer fashions or Italian suits at costs of $1,000, $1,500 and even $3,500. Others spend on season tickets for sports, entertainment and art… or make major investments in redesigning homes or apartments.

With the above in mind, you should determine what priority your career search has… and just how much is at stake on your next career move.

Naturally, we are each in a different career situation. One person may be 28… another 63. We all have different amounts of career earnings ahead of us, but that is one way to judge the importance of the move.

Do you have $300,000… $1,000,000 or $2,000,000 worth of earnings left in your career? Or, perhaps it is $3,000,000 to $10,000,000? Clearly, for most people there is considerable future income at stake. If this is your case, then your career advancement should be given priority at this time.

Keep in mind the long term value of improving your situation. When people make a good career move *(a move to a better job, with a good firm, and in a growing industry)*… they normally maintain the increase over where they were for many years. Of course, more challenge, satisfaction, pure enjoyment and potential are real "value factors" as well.

Whatever your decision about how aggressively you will search, I know you will benefit from *The 15 New Rules For Job Hunting Success*. I've tried to make them as simple and straightforward as possible. They all won't be relevant to your situation, but if you follow the ones that are— your confidence will soar and you'll be on your way. *With best wishes for your success.*

Bob Gerberg

Some preliminary comments

On technology
Technology has made job hunting an entirely new ball game...
unimaginable just five years ago.

On industry change
Changes in the past were made by luck or circumstance. Today
changing industries can be under your control.

On growth firms
Growth industries and fast growing firms are where the action
is... and there is often far less competition, as well.

On being unemployed
A common perception: employers feel that good talent doesn't
last long in the market. So, get into action—fast.

On age barriers
Age is not the barrier that you may think. Veteran talent is
always valued. The key is knowing how to market yourself.

On getting market coverage
You want maximum exposure during the time you are in the
market. Why settle for 2% when 85% is now possible?

On marketing vs. job hunting
Marketing yourself isn't just selling factual credentials. You
need to sell transferable skills— and to the right people. Engage in job hunting the way you used to, and you'll experience
months of trial and error and frustration.

On being aggressive
If you had a valuable piece of art to auction at Christie's in
New York, would you prefer 15 or 25 bidders, or just 1 or 2?

On old resume formulas
They don't work, because of the volume of resumes which are now mailed, faxed or emailed—or simply left posted online.

On narrative presentation
The C-Level biography, a little-understood resume approach, can give any executive a powerful advantage.

On recruiters and Venture Capitalists
For people with good tickets, placing a significant number of resumes with recruiters and VCs can be very productive.

On privacy issues and the Internet
Improperly revealing details can come back to haunt you for many years—because of resume scanning.

On selecting references
What your references may say is important, but their enthusiasm and conviction is much more important.

On creating your own job
The more senior you are, the more likely your next position will be created for you. You just need to know how to do it.

On contacting employers directly
It's difficult to do right. But, direct mail with the right message... told to the right employers... can be very effective.

On negotiating
Many people get initial offers raised by 10% to 30%... and some achieve cash signing bonuses from $7,500 to $100,000.

This system is based upon
the principle that successful
job hunting depends 70%
on personal marketing
and 30% on credentials.
It's also about mastering the
personal marketing process.
Once you do, you'll be in
control of your career destiny.

RULE #1

Aggressively Compete in All
8 Segments of Today's Job Market.

All market segments are avenues to opportunities. Exposure in each of them will give you many more options.

The job market has changed more in the last five years than in the previous 50. With today's competition, you need to plan on generating a lot of interest in your talents.

Employment experts all agree that it is more important than ever to really market yourself. Today, superior marketing distinguishes America's top firms, including PepsiCo, IBM, J & J and others. A *Harvard Business Review* cover story put it most appropriately. It was called "Marketing Is Everything." Our philosophy is based on the same principles. Aggressive marketing will be your key to job hunting success.

Whether you're a CEO or a young salesperson, you need to identify your right market and clarify your goals in terms of job titles and industries. Then you need to be "packaged" with superior resumes and letters.

Once you have them, you need to be "promoted" wisely and enough to put yourself in the driver's seat. This means you must be able to access the market... having information at your fingertips about the openings, leads and contacts relating to opportunities right for you.

Can traditional job hunting methods still work? Obviously, the answer is yes. If you are willing to take long enough and knock on enough doors, you'll eventually get a job. But what kind of job?... And for what income? Will it be the right career move?... And how long will it have taken you? These are things you need to seriously consider.

How The Published Job Market Works

The market consists of employers who make public their openings… and those who don't. There are five segments to the published job market. Through our Job Market Access Center, clients can connect with openings in each segment.

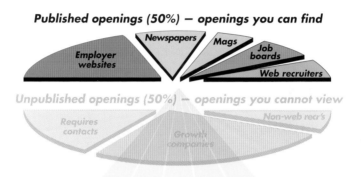

The vast majority of the published portion of the job market is available through these sources.

100,000	3,000	2,100	300	3,500
Employers	**Newspapers**	**Trade Mag's**	**Job Boards**	**Recruiters**

We believe in an aggressive philosophy that is targeted at the development of 3 to 4 interview possibilities from each of the 8 market segments described above and on the adjacent page. This may sound like a lot, but you have to be realistic about rejections. By developing this level of activity, you increase your chances of having several offers mature at the same time.

How The Unpublished Job Market Works

Through our Job Market Access Center we also help you compete in the unpublished job market. Here we use the top databases and unique technology to help clients take the actions indicated in the illustration below.

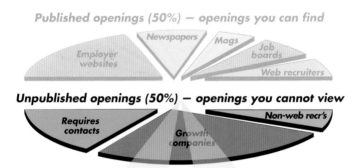

Published openings (50%) — openings you can find

Newspapers Mags Job boards Employer websites Web recruiters

Unpublished openings (50%) — openings you cannot view

Requires contacts Growth companies Non-web recr's

You can compete in the unpublished market... and uncover openings by taking all or some of the following actions.

Contacting firms receiving venture capital	Direct mail to decision makers in medium-sized employers
Direct mail to decision makers at large employers	Networking industry leaders
Contacting influential alumni	Networking existing contacts
Direct mail to decision makers in growth firms	Using breaking news to uncover emerging jobs

Getting a regular stream of several interviews... every week for 8 to 10 weeks can guarantee the success of most people.

To do it, you'll need to compete in all market segments.

How McKenzie Scott helps with rule #1
Aggressively compete in all
8 segments of today's job market

To help you compete in all eight segments of the market, we market you to recruiters, growth firms, large employers and venture capitalists. And, our Job Market Access Center provides instant connections to openings... leads to openings... and potential contacts.

RULE #2

Don't Proceed Without Pinpointing
Your Job Hunting Goals.

**Many people have marketable assets and skills...
but fail to go after the right occupations and job titles.**

It may surprise you, but many people pursue the wrong job titles. However, if their transferable skills are clarified, they can be repositioned for different goals, and sometimes for much more advancement than they thought possible. Regardless of your most recent position, you need to think of yourself as "one of a kind" and to present yourself accordingly.

We all have seen career fields change dramatically over a decade. Fields that once offered great opportunity have become financially confining with limited growth possibilities.

Does print advertising offer the same career possibilities as it did a decade ago? Does selling in the steel industry? Does being a doctor who is a general practitioner? Career fields change at a much faster pace than most people realize.

Experience has proven that if you take a narrow view of yourself, you could be making a major mistake. For example, if you see yourself as a specialist (i.e., a banker), you may believe you are locked into a given career. On the other hand, you may feel you have few options because you are too much of a generalist.

Believe it or not, there are 22,000 different job titles in use today, but 95% of all professionals fall within one of several hundred career specialties which are usually in significant demand. So, try to decide on your right career goals. And, you'll improve your chances by pursuing titles that the market makes available in abundance.

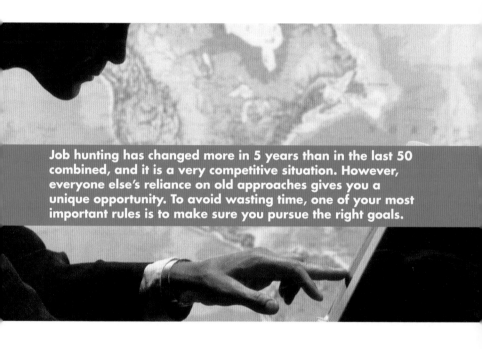

Job hunting has changed more in 5 years than in the last 50 combined, and it is a very competitive situation. However, everyone else's reliance on old approaches gives you a unique opportunity. To avoid wasting time, one of your most important rules is to make sure you pursue the right goals.

People select new careers based on one motivating factor... or several factors:

■ Your previous experience may be related;
■ You may have knowledge through education;
■ Knowledge may exist from outside interests;
■ Your choices may be based on transferable skills.

The 400 most popular occupations... where do you fit... and do any others interest you?

Occupations below are listed generically... and do not necessarily refer to the level of job title that you might seek... e.g., we have listed Marketing Director. Your goal might be Marketing Manager, VP Marketing, Sr. VP Marketing or Chief Marketing Officer. Based on the color coding at the top of this page... check any fields you might want to explore.

❏❏❏❏ Airline Pilot	❏❏❏❏ Astronomer
❏❏❏❏ Academic Team	❏❏❏❏ Athletic Coach
❏❏❏❏ Accountant	❏❏❏❏ Auditor
❏❏❏❏ Account Executive	❏❏❏❏ Author
❏❏❏❏ Actor	❏❏❏❏ Baker
❏❏❏❏ Actuary	❏❏❏❏ Banker
❏❏❏❏ Acquisition Analyst	❏❏❏❏ Bankruptcy Attorney
❏❏❏❏ Administrative Asst.	❏❏❏❏ Benefits Manager
❏❏❏❏ Administrative Analyst	❏❏❏❏ Biologist
❏❏❏❏ Administrator	❏❏❏❏ Bio-feedback Specialist
❏❏❏❏ Advertising Director	❏❏❏❏ Biomedical Engineer
❏❏❏❏ Aerospace Engineer	❏❏❏❏ Biotechnical Researcher
❏❏❏❏ Agent	❏❏❏❏ Broadcaster
❏❏❏❏ Agricultural Inspector	❏❏❏❏ Broker
❏❏❏❏ Agricultural Scientist	❏❏❏❏ Building Manager
❏❏❏❏ Air Traffic Controller	❏❏❏❏ Building Contractor
❏❏❏❏ Animal Trainer	❏❏❏❏ Building Inspector
❏❏❏❏ Anthropologist	❏❏❏❏ Business Analyst
❏❏❏❏ Appraiser	❏❏❏❏ Business Planner
❏❏❏❏ Architect	❏❏❏❏ Business Manager
❏❏❏❏ Art Director	❏❏❏❏ Buyer
❏❏❏❏ Artist	❏❏❏❏ Call Center Manager

❑ ❑ ❑ ❑ Career Counselor
❑ ❑ ❑ ❑ Cash Manager
❑ ❑ ❑ ❑ Ceramic Engineer
❑ ❑ ❑ ❑ CEO / COO / CAO
❑ ❑ ❑ ❑ Chef
❑ ❑ ❑ ❑ Chemical Dept. Spec.
❑ ❑ ❑ ❑ Chemical Engineer
❑ ❑ ❑ ❑ Chemist
❑ ❑ ❑ ❑ Child Care Manager
❑ ❑ ❑ ❑ Chief Medical Officer
❑ ❑ ❑ ❑ Chiropractor
❑ ❑ ❑ ❑ Cinematographer
❑ ❑ ❑ ❑ City Housing Manager
❑ ❑ ❑ ❑ City Manager
❑ ❑ ❑ ❑ Civil Engineer
❑ ❑ ❑ ❑ Claims Manager
❑ ❑ ❑ ❑ Clinical Research Asst.
❑ ❑ ❑ ❑ Collections Manager
❑ ❑ ❑ ❑ Compliance Manager
❑ ❑ ❑ ❑ Comptroller
❑ ❑ ❑ ❑ Computer Manager
❑ ❑ ❑ ❑ Commercial Artist
❑ ❑ ❑ ❑ Commun. Affairs Director
❑ ❑ ❑ ❑ Communications Director
❑ ❑ ❑ ❑ Communications Engineer
❑ ❑ ❑ ❑ Compensation Analyst
❑ ❑ ❑ ❑ Computer Programmer
❑ ❑ ❑ ❑ Computer Ops. Manager
❑ ❑ ❑ ❑ Computer Engineer
❑ ❑ ❑ ❑ Computer Operator
❑ ❑ ❑ ❑ Computer Graphics Spec.
❑ ❑ ❑ ❑ Construction Engineer
❑ ❑ ❑ ❑ Construction Manager
❑ ❑ ❑ ❑ Consultant
❑ ❑ ❑ ❑ Consumer Relations Mgr.
❑ ❑ ❑ ❑ Contract Administrator
❑ ❑ ❑ ❑ Copyright Attorney
❑ ❑ ❑ ❑ Copywriter
❑ ❑ ❑ ❑ Corporate Planner
❑ ❑ ❑ ❑ Corrections Officer
❑ ❑ ❑ ❑ Cosmetologist
❑ ❑ ❑ ❑ Credit Analyst
❑ ❑ ❑ ❑ Cruise Director

❑ ❑ ❑ ❑ CTO / CIO
❑ ❑ ❑ ❑ Customer Service Mgr.
❑ ❑ ❑ ❑ Cryptologist
❑ ❑ ❑ ❑ Dancer
❑ ❑ ❑ ❑ Data Security Mgr.
❑ ❑ ❑ ❑ Database Manager
❑ ❑ ❑ ❑ Day Care Instructor
❑ ❑ ❑ ❑ Dentist
❑ ❑ ❑ ❑ Designer
❑ ❑ ❑ ❑ Design Engineer
❑ ❑ ❑ ❑ Desktop Publisher
❑ ❑ ❑ ❑ Developer
❑ ❑ ❑ ❑ Development Officer
❑ ❑ ❑ ❑ Diamond Merchant
❑ ❑ ❑ ❑ Dietitian
❑ ❑ ❑ ❑ Direct Marketer
❑ ❑ ❑ ❑ Director
❑ ❑ ❑ ❑ Distribution Manager
❑ ❑ ❑ ❑ Diversity Manager
❑ ❑ ❑ ❑ Economist
❑ ❑ ❑ ❑ EEO Compliance Mgr.
❑ ❑ ❑ ❑ Editor
❑ ❑ ❑ ❑ Education Admin'r
❑ ❑ ❑ ❑ Electrical Engineer
❑ ❑ ❑ ❑ Electro Optical Engineer
❑ ❑ ❑ ❑ Electronics Engineer
❑ ❑ ❑ ❑ Embassy Management
❑ ❑ ❑ ❑ Employment Agent
❑ ❑ ❑ ❑ Engineer Technician
❑ ❑ ❑ ❑ Entrepreneur
❑ ❑ ❑ ❑ Environmental Analyst
❑ ❑ ❑ ❑ Environmental Attorney
❑ ❑ ❑ ❑ Environmental Engineer
❑ ❑ ❑ ❑ Environmental Spec't
❑ ❑ ❑ ❑ Escrow Officer
❑ ❑ ❑ ❑ Estimator
❑ ❑ ❑ ❑ Executive Assistant
❑ ❑ ❑ ❑ Executive Director
❑ ❑ ❑ ❑ Executive Recruiter
❑ ❑ ❑ ❑ Facilities Manager
❑ ❑ ❑ ❑ Family Counselor
❑ ❑ ❑ ❑ Fashion Events Mgr.
❑ ❑ ❑ ❑ Fashion Merchandiser

❏ ❏ ❏ ❏ Fast Food Manager
❏ ❏ ❏ ❏ Film Producer
❏ ❏ ❏ ❏ Film Production Asst.
❏ ❏ ❏ ❏ Financial Analyst
❏ ❏ ❏ ❏ Financial Planner
❏ ❏ ❏ ❏ Financier
❏ ❏ ❏ ❏ Fine Artist
❏ ❏ ❏ ❏ Fish / Wildlife Specialist
❏ ❏ ❏ ❏ Fitness Consultant
❏ ❏ ❏ ❏ Flight Attendant
❏ ❏ ❏ ❏ Flight Engineer
❏ ❏ ❏ ❏ Floral Designer
❏ ❏ ❏ ❏ Food & Beverage Dir.
❏ ❏ ❏ ❏ Food Service Manager
❏ ❏ ❏ ❏ Forestry Technician
❏ ❏ ❏ ❏ Franchise Management
❏ ❏ ❏ ❏ Franchise Sales
❏ ❏ ❏ ❏ Fraud Investigator
❏ ❏ ❏ ❏ Freelance Writer
❏ ❏ ❏ ❏ Fundraiser
❏ ❏ ❏ ❏ Funeral Director
❏ ❏ ❏ ❏ General Manager
❏ ❏ ❏ ❏ Geologist
❏ ❏ ❏ ❏ General Counsel
❏ ❏ ❏ ❏ Geriatric Specialist
❏ ❏ ❏ ❏ Gerontologist
❏ ❏ ❏ ❏ Glamour Photographer
❏ ❏ ❏ ❏ Golf Club Manager
❏ ❏ ❏ ❏ Gourmet Chef
❏ ❏ ❏ ❏ Graphic Designer
❏ ❏ ❏ ❏ Grounds Keeper
❏ ❏ ❏ ❏ Hazardous Waste Mgr.
❏ ❏ ❏ ❏ Health Care Manager
❏ ❏ ❏ ❏ Health Therapist
❏ ❏ ❏ ❏ Health Service Admin'r
❏ ❏ ❏ ❏ Hearing Officer
❏ ❏ ❏ ❏ HMO Administrator
❏ ❏ ❏ ❏ Home Economist
❏ ❏ ❏ ❏ Horticulturist
❏ ❏ ❏ ❏ Hospital Administrator
❏ ❏ ❏ ❏ Hotel Manager
❏ ❏ ❏ ❏ HR Manager
❏ ❏ ❏ ❏ Importer
❏ ❏ ❏ ❏ Industrial Designer
❏ ❏ ❏ ❏ Industrial Engineer

❏ ❏ ❏ ❏ Information Director
❏ ❏ ❏ ❏ Inside Sales
❏ ❏ ❏ ❏ Insurance Adjuster
❏ ❏ ❏ ❏ Interior Decorator
❏ ❏ ❏ ❏ Internal Controls Dir.
❏ ❏ ❏ ❏ International Acct.
❏ ❏ ❏ ❏ International Courier
❏ ❏ ❏ ❏ International Lawyer
❏ ❏ ❏ ❏ Interpreter
❏ ❏ ❏ ❏ Investigator
❏ ❏ ❏ ❏ Investment Banker
❏ ❏ ❏ ❏ Investment Manager
❏ ❏ ❏ ❏ IT Architect
❏ ❏ ❏ ❏ IT Project Manager
❏ ❏ ❏ ❏ IT Systems Analyst
❏ ❏ ❏ ❏ Jeweler
❏ ❏ ❏ ❏ Joint Venture Manager
❏ ❏ ❏ ❏ Journalist
❏ ❏ ❏ ❏ Labor Negotiator
❏ ❏ ❏ ❏ Labor Organizer
❏ ❏ ❏ ❏ Labor Relations Mgr.
❏ ❏ ❏ ❏ Lab Services Director
❏ ❏ ❏ ❏ Lab Technician
❏ ❏ ❏ ❏ Land Developer
❏ ❏ ❏ ❏ Landscape Architect
❏ ❏ ❏ ❏ Law Enforcement Officer
❏ ❏ ❏ ❏ Lawyer
❏ ❏ ❏ ❏ Leasing Manager
❏ ❏ ❏ ❏ Legal Secretary
❏ ❏ ❏ ❏ Library Manager
❏ ❏ ❏ ❏ Litigation Attorney
❏ ❏ ❏ ❏ Loan Officer
❏ ❏ ❏ ❏ Lobbyist
❏ ❏ ❏ ❏ Logistics Manager
❏ ❏ ❏ ❏ Maintenance Manager
❏ ❏ ❏ ❏ Management Consul't
❏ ❏ ❏ ❏ Managed Care Director
❏ ❏ ❏ ❏ Managing Partner
❏ ❏ ❏ ❏ Manufacturing Dir.
❏ ❏ ❏ ❏ Manpower Planner
❏ ❏ ❏ ❏ Marine Biologist
❏ ❏ ❏ ❏ Market Res. Analyst
❏ ❏ ❏ ❏ Marketing Director
❏ ❏ ❏ ❏ Materials Manager
❏ ❏ ❏ ❏ Mathematician

❑ ❑ ❑ ❑ Membership Chairman	❑ ❑ ❑ ❑ Physician
❑ ❑ ❑ ❑ Mechanic	❑ ❑ ❑ ❑ Physician Assistant
❑ ❑ ❑ ❑ Mechanical Engineer	❑ ❑ ❑ ❑ Physicist
❑ ❑ ❑ ❑ Media Buyer	❑ ❑ ❑ ❑ Planning Specialist / Dir.
❑ ❑ ❑ ❑ Medical Investor	❑ ❑ ❑ ❑ Podiatrist
❑ ❑ ❑ ❑ Medical Secretary	❑ ❑ ❑ ❑ Political Analyst
❑ ❑ ❑ ❑ Medical Technician	❑ ❑ ❑ ❑ Political Scientist
❑ ❑ ❑ ❑ Mental Health Coun'r	❑ ❑ ❑ ❑ Politician
❑ ❑ ❑ ❑ Merchandiser	❑ ❑ ❑ ❑ Portfolio Manager
❑ ❑ ❑ ❑ Metallographic Tech'n	❑ ❑ ❑ ❑ Preschool Management
❑ ❑ ❑ ❑ Metallurgical Engin'g	❑ ❑ ❑ ❑ Preschool Teacher
❑ ❑ ❑ ❑ Meteorologist	❑ ❑ ❑ ❑ Principal
❑ ❑ ❑ ❑ Microbiologist	❑ ❑ ❑ ❑ Private Banker
❑ ❑ ❑ ❑ MIS Manager	❑ ❑ ❑ ❑ Private Investigator
❑ ❑ ❑ ❑ Motion Picture Director	❑ ❑ ❑ ❑ Probation Officer
❑ ❑ ❑ ❑ Motivational Speaker	❑ ❑ ❑ ❑ Process Engineer
❑ ❑ ❑ ❑ Multimedia Director	❑ ❑ ❑ ❑ Producer
❑ ❑ ❑ ❑ Musician	❑ ❑ ❑ ❑ Product/ Brand Mgr.
❑ ❑ ❑ ❑ Network Administrator	❑ ❑ ❑ ❑ Product Engineer
❑ ❑ ❑ ❑ Network Specialist	❑ ❑ ❑ ❑ Production Engineer
❑ ❑ ❑ ❑ Network Operator	❑ ❑ ❑ ❑ Production Planner
❑ ❑ ❑ ❑ New Product Mgr.	❑ ❑ ❑ ❑ Professional Athlete
❑ ❑ ❑ ❑ Novelist	❑ ❑ ❑ ❑ Professional Coach
❑ ❑ ❑ ❑ Nuclear Engineer	❑ ❑ ❑ ❑ Professor
❑ ❑ ❑ ❑ Nuclear Specialist	❑ ❑ ❑ ❑ Project Engineer
❑ ❑ ❑ ❑ Nutritionist	❑ ❑ ❑ ❑ Project Manager
❑ ❑ ❑ ❑ Nursing Administrator	❑ ❑ ❑ ❑ Program Manager
❑ ❑ ❑ ❑ Occup. Therapist	❑ ❑ ❑ ❑ Property Manager
❑ ❑ ❑ ❑ Oceanographer	❑ ❑ ❑ ❑ Public Administrator
❑ ❑ ❑ ❑ Office Manager	❑ ❑ ❑ ❑ Public Safety Director
❑ ❑ ❑ ❑ Operations Manager	❑ ❑ ❑ ❑ PR Specialist
❑ ❑ ❑ ❑ Operations Research Dir.	❑ ❑ ❑ ❑ Publisher
❑ ❑ ❑ ❑ Optical Technician	❑ ❑ ❑ ❑ Purchasing Agent
❑ ❑ ❑ ❑ Optometrist	❑ ❑ ❑ ❑ Publishing Director
❑ ❑ ❑ ❑ Organiz'l Devel't Mgr.	❑ ❑ ❑ ❑ Quality Assurance Spec't
❑ ❑ ❑ ❑ Outplacement Spec't	❑ ❑ ❑ ❑ Quality Control Engineer
❑ ❑ ❑ ❑ Paralegal	❑ ❑ ❑ ❑ Quality Control Inspector
❑ ❑ ❑ ❑ Park Ranger	❑ ❑ ❑ ❑ Rabbi / Minister / Priest
❑ ❑ ❑ ❑ Patent Attorney	❑ ❑ ❑ ❑ Radio / TV Announcer
❑ ❑ ❑ ❑ Payroll Specialist	❑ ❑ ❑ ❑ Radiologic Technician
❑ ❑ ❑ ❑ Personnel Specialist	❑ ❑ ❑ ❑ Radiology Manager
❑ ❑ ❑ ❑ Petroleum Engineer	❑ ❑ ❑ ❑ Railroad Engineer
❑ ❑ ❑ ❑ Pharmacist	❑ ❑ ❑ ❑ Real Estate Broker
❑ ❑ ❑ ❑ Photographer	❑ ❑ ❑ ❑ Recreational Director
❑ ❑ ❑ ❑ Physical Therapist	❑ ❑ ❑ ❑ Recruiter

- ❏ ❏ ❏ ❏ Redevelopment Specialist
- ❏ ❏ ❏ ❏ Regulatory Affairs Mgr.
- ❏ ❏ ❏ ❏ Registered Nurse
- ❏ ❏ ❏ ❏ Rehabilitation Counselor
- ❏ ❏ ❏ ❏ Relocation Manager
- ❏ ❏ ❏ ❏ Reporter
- ❏ ❏ ❏ ❏ R & D Manager
- ❏ ❏ ❏ ❏ Research Specialist
- ❏ ❏ ❏ ❏ Restaurant Manager
- ❏ ❏ ❏ ❏ Retail Store Manager
- ❏ ❏ ❏ ❏ Risk Analyst
- ❏ ❏ ❏ ❏ Safety Engineer
- ❏ ❏ ❏ ❏ Sales Engineer
- ❏ ❏ ❏ ❏ Sales Trainer
- ❏ ❏ ❏ ❏ Sales Promotion Mgr.
- ❏ ❏ ❏ ❏ Sales Representative
- ❏ ❏ ❏ ❏ Sales Manager
- ❏ ❏ ❏ ❏ Service Manager
- ❏ ❏ ❏ ❏ Sanitation Engineer
- ❏ ❏ ❏ ❏ Scientific Programmer
- ❏ ❏ ❏ ❏ Scientific Writer
- ❏ ❏ ❏ ❏ Securities Analyst
- ❏ ❏ ❏ ❏ Security Consultant
- ❏ ❏ ❏ ❏ Security Director
- ❏ ❏ ❏ ❏ Seminar Presenter
- ❏ ❏ ❏ ❏ Ship's Officer
- ❏ ❏ ❏ ❏ Singer
- ❏ ❏ ❏ ❏ Social Director
- ❏ ❏ ❏ ❏ Social Program Planner
- ❏ ❏ ❏ ❏ Social Research
- ❏ ❏ ❏ ❏ Social Scientist
- ❏ ❏ ❏ ❏ Social Worker
- ❏ ❏ ❏ ❏ Sociologist
- ❏ ❏ ❏ ❏ Software Developer
- ❏ ❏ ❏ ❏ Software Engineer
- ❏ ❏ ❏ ❏ Soil Scientist
- ❏ ❏ ❏ ❏ Special Events Mgr.
- ❏ ❏ ❏ ❏ Special Education Teacher
- ❏ ❏ ❏ ❏ Special Projects Director
- ❏ ❏ ❏ ❏ Speech Pathologist
- ❏ ❏ ❏ ❏ Speech Writer
- ❏ ❏ ❏ ❏ Sports Event Manager
- ❏ ❏ ❏ ❏ Statistician

- ❏ ❏ ❏ ❏ Store Manager
- ❏ ❏ ❏ ❏ Strategic Alliance Dir.
- ❏ ❏ ❏ ❏ Strategic Planning Dir.
- ❏ ❏ ❏ ❏ Stress Reduction Spec't
- ❏ ❏ ❏ ❏ Stockbroker
- ❏ ❏ ❏ ❏ Surveyor
- ❏ ❏ ❏ ❏ Structural Engineer
- ❏ ❏ ❏ ❏ Superintendent
- ❏ ❏ ❏ ❏ Supply Chain Director
- ❏ ❏ ❏ ❏ System Engineer
- ❏ ❏ ❏ ❏ Systems Analyst
- ❏ ❏ ❏ ❏ Systems Programmer
- ❏ ❏ ❏ ❏ System Administrator
- ❏ ❏ ❏ ❏ Tax Specialist
- ❏ ❏ ❏ ❏ Teacher
- ❏ ❏ ❏ ❏ Technical Support Spec't
- ❏ ❏ ❏ ❏ Technical Illustrator
- ❏ ❏ ❏ ❏ Technical Writer
- ❏ ❏ ❏ ❏ Technology Director
- ❏ ❏ ❏ ❏ Telecom Analyst
- ❏ ❏ ❏ ❏ Telemarketer
- ❏ ❏ ❏ ❏ Theatrical Director
- ❏ ❏ ❏ ❏ Title Examiner
- ❏ ❏ ❏ ❏ Tour Escort
- ❏ ❏ ❏ ❏ Tour Guide Director
- ❏ ❏ ❏ ❏ Traffic Manager
- ❏ ❏ ❏ ❏ Trainer Translator
- ❏ ❏ ❏ ❏ Transportation Mgr.
- ❏ ❏ ❏ ❏ Travel Agent
- ❏ ❏ ❏ ❏ Treasurer
- ❏ ❏ ❏ ❏ Tree Surgeon
- ❏ ❏ ❏ ❏ TV Programmer
- ❏ ❏ ❏ ❏ Underwriter
- ❏ ❏ ❏ ❏ Union Representative
- ❏ ❏ ❏ ❏ Univ. Administrator
- ❏ ❏ ❏ ❏ University Dean
- ❏ ❏ ❏ ❏ Urban Planner
- ❏ ❏ ❏ ❏ Veterinarian
- ❏ ❏ ❏ ❏ Vendor Relations Director
- ❏ ❏ ❏ ❏ Viticulturist
- ❏ ❏ ❏ ❏ Warehouse Manager
- ❏ ❏ ❏ ❏ Weapons Expert

The 5 Most Popular Total Career Changes

Some less conventional moves that may represent a whole new direction. Do any interest you?

1. Do you want to be a consultant?

The field has continually expanded at a rapid rate. If you decide to become a practicing consultant, your perceived professionalism will be very important.

Thousands of people begin thriving consulting practices each year. Recognize that you will need some form of specialty if you are to get off to a fast start. For those attracted to consulting, remember, the knowledge you have to offer must somehow be sold. Success rests squarely on your ability to attract and keep clients. However, the biggest reason for failure is that people don't foresee the selling effort required.

If selling is not your suit, but you feel you have a great deal to offer, you will have to attract one or more partners or employees who will sell your services.

Some of the most popular consulting specialties include finance, marketing, new product development, IT and systems, executive search and outplacement, cost reduction, and public relations. There is also good activity in labor relations, engineering, design, and other technical disciplines.

If you would rather join an existing firm, there are thousands of organizations that can benefit from adding new talent. It is an easier way to get started than striking out on your own, and you can always benefit from the experience.

Regardless of the type of consulting you choose, remember that the special knowledge that makes a consultant valuable today may be obsolete in a few years. So you need to keep current. If you enjoy variety and intellectual challenge, consulting could be your right move.

2. Could you work as a producer?

Producers bring in business. Some examples include executive recruiters, financial planners, stockbrokers, real estate brokers and outplacement specialists. If you have contacts and need a shift, this kind of role can be attractive. There are opportunities for producers in every discipline. The key is to focus on something you can do well.

3. Are you interested in a job where you can make an investment and have some form of ownership?

Some executives have capital and are looking to find an employment opportunity where their efforts and capital can be joined to offer them entrepreneurial rewards.

Perhaps you have some ideas about improving a product or product line that is already being marketed. Or, you may be able to put together financing for a firm's needs. Your ability to raise capital from VCs, private investors or even friends could be critical. These situations are most appealing when your skills complement those who are in a business with promising potential. What's more, you can pick businesses that offer you the degree of involvement that you prefer. For example, opportunities that require limited involvement might include businesses with multiple units of car washes, laundromats, theaters, apartments, and parking lots.

Small chains of specialty stores can also be candidates...
e.g., pet shops, nurseries, sporting goods stores and marinas,
and product lines such as computers, men's clothing or gourmet
foods and wines. Other possibilities include small restaurants
and inns, printing services, and small manufacturing plants.
Many existing businesses have good potential but need talent
and capital to go to the next level. Associating with existing
businesses in real estate may also be suitable... e.g., a company seeking to capitalize on vacant land, small commercial
buildings, single or multiple family residences, abandoned
factories and government repossessions. Employee-investors
have earned millions, but the risks can be high.

4. Are you interested in managing a nonprofit or working in education?

Surprising to some, there are more than 20,000 trade
organizations, and many are exceptionally well-funded. Most
trade associations are run like businesses and have similar
needs. In many respects, education is like any other service
business. People must be recruited and trained, and facilities
must be operated efficiently. Information systems and data
processing are needed; funds must be raised and public relations must be maintained.

Those with corporate experience will find they are of
particular value in the graduate schools of business. In fact,
a number of universities have former corporate officers as
professors, administrators, heads of development and fundraising, and deans of their business schools.

Here, an advanced degree is usually a prerequisite. Those
who favor classroom teaching or lecturing may still find that
they eventually gravitate to management.

5. What about serving on a few boards?

Many executives who can bring prestige and experience to smaller corporations become sought after for directorships. However, it usually takes some planning. When you have served on one board, you will likely be invited to join others. That is particularly true if you have experience that is apparent to nominating committees. In fact, directorships on just three or four corporations, along with committee work, can often provide adequate income and challenge.

Some stock exchanges can direct you to clearinghouse services for executives interested in directorships. It is also possible to run a campaign aimed at existing directors, investment bankers, lawyers, and CEOs by discreetly inquiring whether your services might be valuable to one or more of the companies with which they are associated.

Obviously, this avenue is most feasible for executives with strong reputations. However, even if this is not the case, it is possible to develop opportunities. Think carefully of what you have to offer that would set you apart.

If you are known as an executive who can increase productivity or cut costs, or if you have proven talents in securing financing, making acquisitions, or entering new markets, then it will be easy for many board members and CEOs to envision your contributions.

These openings are usually coordinated by the corporate secretary, who may be a good contact. Because directorships now carry more exposure to liability, corporations no longer expect directors to serve for just a nominal sum or without proper insurance.

You need to pursue goals that are in demand, and that will advance you to the next level. If you do, and market yourself aggressively, moving up may be easier than you realize.

How McKenzie Scott helps with rule #2
Don't proceed without pinpointing
your job hunting goals

When you complete our profiles, they will surface all of your historical experiences, accomplishments and transferable skills in a highly organized way. The information you provide is supplemented by a teleconference review and our marketability evaluation. Our staff team then analyzes all the information we have and recommends appropriate goals.

RULE #3

Expand Your Marketability... Far
Beyond Your Factual Credentials.

Besides your factual credentials, you'll want to identify and market key phrases that describe your transferable skills.

The new job market is so competitive you'll need to do more than just present your background. Don't trap yourself by thinking, *"This is simply who I am, where I've been and what I've done."* People fail because they never surface and communicate all that is marketable about themselves... and they never build their appeal beyond factual credentials.

Your starting point is to organize your lifetime of experiences. Whether you are a young attorney or a company president, there is probably much more to your story than meets the eye. Organizing past experiences and achievements will reveal insights that can help build your appeal.

Experience has proven that many people never identify 50% of their own assets, simply because they're so close to their own situation. We've learned that most people need to identify 10 to 20 skills which, if properly communicated, can make a major difference in their career opportunities.

Each year, about 20% of the clients who come to us have settled for less, simply because they are not able to communicate their real skills. For example, one client was earning a $65,000 base after almost 20 years. Three years later, she is earning $180,000. Another executive came to us at $125,000. Three years later, he is a CEO at many times that amount. The key in both situations was to market their true assets.

Now, if you are like most people, you can increase your chances through a very simple rule. It has been said time and again by psychologists, spiritual leaders and coaches that the most restrictive limits you face are those you put on yourself. So, don't put any limits on your thinking.

Your knowledge and personality are marketable

Do you have knowledge of a job, a product, a process or a market... from work, hobbies, alumni relationships, research or suppliers? If so, it may be marketable.

Personality, of course, is just a word for that combination of traits that either attracts us to someone, or leaves us unimpressed. More employment decisions are based on personality and chemistry than any other factor. For example: *"He's certainly professional and quick-thinking. I like him, and better yet, I trust him. He'll fit in with our team. I need to get him into the firm."* The perception of your personality has to do with your interest and enthusiasm. How many people get hired because they showed real interest? *A lot!*

Your transferable skills are marketable

Identifying transferable skills is critical (for example, organizing, group presentation skills, problem solving and so on). Today, employers place a premium on men and women who can move from challenge to challenge, handling assignments that draw upon different skills.

Naturally, your experience can also be reviewed according to various "functions" that apply to most businesses, such as sales, production, accounting, marketing and human resources. All areas in which you have knowledge must be identified. At the same time, you need to think of your experience in terms of "action words" that describe what you did, and then translate those activities into achievements, i.e., *controlled, wrote, reshaped,* etc.

Leadership qualities are marketable

If there is one quality you want to communicate, it is leadership ability. Experts say that leaders possess and communicate real convictions—strong feelings and principles that have grown with them over time.

Leadership is also attributed to those who create an image of operating at the far edge of the frontier... into new products, new services and new solutions. We expect our leaders to have the vision and talent to develop new things.

Another skill common to most leaders is their ability to assemble teams and to motivate them to peak achievement. Often creative, intuitive and passionate, they project integrity and trust. If you possess these traits, all of them should be marketed. Image, attitude and presence also play a role.

We've learned that the more ways you can describe your experience, the more you will qualify for jobs in many industries. All organizations are involved in similar functions.

Here are 200+ skills and experience factors you can market... and that employers want. Which apply to you?

SKILLS & CAPABILITIES

- ❏ Ability to get things done quickly
- ❏ Action-oriented
- ❏ Ambitious
- ❏ Analyze situations rapidly
- ❏ Astute researcher
- ❏ Bring order out of chaos
- ❏ Bring out creativity in others
- ❏ Broad administrative skills
- ❏ Consistently find new alternatives
- ❏ Conceptual thinker
- ❏ Contacts at highest levels
- ❏ Creative
- ❏ Decisive
- ❏ Diplomatic
- ❏ Direct large meetings skillfully
- ❏ Drive "out-of-box" thinking
- ❏ Easily win people's confidence
- ❏ Effective at dealing with the public
- ❏ Effective at organizing labor
- ❏ Effective moderator and mediator
- ❏ Enterprising / dynamic
- ❏ Entrepreneurial strengths
- ❏ Excellent recruiter
- ❏ Excellent trainer
- ❏ Exceptional people skills
- ❏ Exceptional team player
- ❏ Flair for putting on events
- ❏ Genuine & sincere
- ❏ Grasp technical matters quickly
- ❏ Handle rapid change easily
- ❏ Hands on / shirt sleeve
- ❏ High achiever / gives 100%
- ❏ High energy / enthusiastic
- ❏ Highly articulate
- ❏ Highly charismatic
- ❏ Highly competitive
- ❏ Highly professional
- ❏ Highly social / outgoing
- ❏ Highly organized
- ❏ In-depth technical knowledge

Also keep in mind that you will need to back them up... with stories and examples

- ❏ Industry leader
- ❏ Innovator / imaginative
- ❏ Inspire others to top performance
- ❏ Instincts for what will sell
- ❏ Introduce change smoothly
- ❏ Intuitive decision maker
- ❏ Know international markets
- ❏ Knowledge of key markets
- ❏ Likable, friendly
- ❏ Loyal
- ❏ Make forceful group presentations
- ❏ Meet demanding objectives
- ❏ Motivator
- ❏ Natural leader
- ❏ Operations-oriented
- ❏ Perfectionist
- ❏ Perform against tight deadlines
- ❏ Persistent
- ❏ Personal contacts for new business
- ❏ Plan major conferences
- ❏ Precise thinker, logical
- ❏ Problem solver
- ❏ Proven record of success
- ❏ Public speaker
- ❏ Quick thinker
- ❏ Recognized authority in my area
- ❏ Relate easily to people at all levels
- ❏ Reliable / responsible
- ❏ Remain calm under pressure
- ❏ Resourceful
- ❏ Risk taker
- ❏ Seasoned competitor
- ❏ Self-motivated
- ❏ Sense of command
- ❏ Sense of humor
- ❏ Shirt-sleeve approach / hands-on
- ❏ Simplify complex problems
- ❏ Skilled at governmental affairs
- ❏ Skilled at union relations
- ❏ Skillful / seasoned negotiator
- ❏ Sophisticated

- ❏ Source of ideas that work
- ❏ Special visual and design taste
- ❏ Strong at consumer selling
- ❏ Strong at corporate selling
- ❏ Strong executive image / presence
- ❏ Strong group communicator
- ❏ Strong social skills
- ❏ Strong theoretical grounding
- ❏ Strong verbal communicator
- ❏ Successfully promote new ideas
- ❏ Superior sales closing skills
- ❏ Superior writing skills
- ❏ Synthesize diverse ideas
- ❏ Tactician / strategic thinker
- ❏ Troubleshooter / problem solver
- ❏ Verbally persuasive / compelling
- ❏ Versatile
- ❏ Very personable & good natured
- ❏ Very positive / upbeat
- ❏ Visionary
- ❏ Well respected
- ❏ Willing to try new approaches
- ❏ Win cooperation at all levels
- ❏ Work alone or as part of a team

EXPERIENCE FACTORS

- ❏ Achievements in international
- ❏ Acquired operations
- ❏ Aggressively managed new inventories
- ❏ Applied leading-edge technologies
- ❏ Authored major business plans
- ❏ Avoided chapter 11 filings
- ❏ Built cross functional teams
- ❏ Built loyal teams
- ❏ Built self-sustaining teams
- ❏ Built strong marketing alliances
- ❏ Built strong technical alliances
- ❏ Chaired civic or social organizations
- ❏ Chaired multifunctional teams
- ❏ Closed millions in consumer sales
- ❏ Closed millions in corporate business

- ❏ Closed under-performing operations
- ❏ Coached winning teams
- ❏ Conceived innovative promotions
- ❏ Conducted major seminars and conferences
- ❏ Consulting firm experience
- ❏ Corporate officer level achievements
- ❏ Designed efficient systems
- ❏ Developed strategic alliances
- ❏ Developed new systems
- ❏ Directed diversification
- ❏ Directed startup
- ❏ Division officer level achievements
- ❏ Enhanced corporate image
- ❏ Entrepreneurial experience
- ❏ Established new standards
- ❏ Experience with market leader
- ❏ Experienced at change management
- ❏ Experienced at cost control
- ❏ Experienced in growth firms
- ❏ Experienced with regulatory agencies
- ❏ Formulated top policies
- ❏ Fortune 1000 experience
- ❏ Handled strategic planning
- ❏ Have had P&L responsibility
- ❏ Helped clients grow revenues
- ❏ High tech experience
- ❏ Implemented sweeping changes
- ❏ Improved customer relations
- ❏ Improved productivity
- ❏ Improved sales / profits
- ❏ Increased shareholder value
- ❏ Installed superior controls
- ❏ Integrated new technologies
- ❏ Joint venture experience
- ❏ Large material responsibilities

To expand your marketability beyond your credentials, you have to sell what employers are BUYING! As discussed, besides credentials they think in terms of phrases that people associate with solving problems or capitalizing on opportunities.

- ❏ Led major expansion
- ❏ Long range planning experience
- ❏ Made go / no-go decisions
- ❏ Managed a large downsizing
- ❏ Managed a lot of people
- ❏ Managed a successful operation
- ❏ Managed complex operations
- ❏ Managed large budgets
- ❏ Managed large investment portfolios
- ❏ Managed rapid growth
- ❏ Managed succession planning
- ❏ Manufacturing experience
- ❏ Minimized liability exposure
- ❏ Minimized litigation
- ❏ Modernized manufacturing
- ❏ Multi-plant experience
- ❏ Multi-product / multi-market experience
- ❏ Large company experience
- ❏ Negotiated foreign contracts
- ❏ Negotiated mergers or acquisitions
- ❏ Negotiated major deals
- ❏ Nonprofit experience
- ❏ Opened new markets
- ❏ Opened new plants
- ❏ Orchestrated major change
- ❏ Overhauled ineffective methods
- ❏ Overhauled vendor relationships
- ❏ Participated in a breakthrough
- ❏ Patent / invention holder
- ❏ Planned fundraising programs
- ❏ Private company experience
- ❏ Procured major funds, grants
- ❏ Project management experience
- ❏ Public company experience
- ❏ Published author of articles
- ❏ Published author of books
- ❏ Recapitalized organization
- ❏ Recovered tax payments
- ❏ Recruited top performers
- ❏ Recruited substantial volunteers
- ❏ Re-engineered processes
- ❏ Reorganized and revitalized
- ❏ Restructured debt
- ❏ Revamped operations
- ❏ Revamped supply chain
- ❏ Salvaged unprofitable operations
- ❏ Served on civic boards
- ❏ Served on corporate boards
- ❏ Served on key committees
- ❏ Served on nonprofit boards
- ❏ Service firm experience
- ❏ Skilled at crisis management
- ❏ Skilled at outsourcing
- ❏ Sold off undesirable properties
- ❏ Started prototype operations
- ❏ Streamlined processes
- ❏ Substantial line experience
- ❏ Substantial staff experience
- ❏ Substantial startup experience
- ❏ Succeeded in declining market
- ❏ Succeeded where others failed
- ❏ Ten+ years experience
- ❏ Top management experience
- ❏ Turned around operations
- ❏ Twenty+ years experience
- ❏ Upgraded investor relations
- ❏ Work a 60+ hour week
- ❏ Worked closely with top mgmt.

A select number of key phrases should be communicated in all your resumes and letters... and used throughout all phone discussions and interviews. When you do this you will expand your marketability... far beyond your factual credentials.

Having a communication strategy... and putting your key phrases into stories.

To appreciate a communication strategy, consider the "platform" of a presidential candidate. It anticipates questions on issues and formulates statements to guide the candidate's answers. Now, when any of us recruit, we have a concept in mind. In the final analysis, we hire others for the skills and abilities that certain key descriptive phrases imply.

To expand your marketability, you must develop stories that incorporate those phrases to create maximum interest. Without stories, most people will forget what you say in a matter of minutes. We all remember good stories. To ensure your points are memorable, we use a method for creating interesting stories. SOAR is an acronym that stands for Situation, Opportunities, Actions and Results. It offers a process for describing your past experience.

Our SOAR process... and how it works

- **Situations.** Describe a job by outlining the situation when you began, making it interesting.

- **Opportunities.** Then describe the opportunities the job presented. For example, "When I joined the firm, sales had been declining for three years. I saw the opportunity to target new areas."

- **Actions.** Next, move to actions taken by you and others (the team). We believe that these actions are the most important part of the SOAR process, and a great place for the descriptive phrases.

- **Results.** Then relate what results occurred. For the "R" in SOAR, try to quantify the results. For example, you cut costs by $100,000 or 20%. In many administrative situations, you can measure results using statements like "*I* *did it in half the time"* or *"The system I developed was adopted throughout the company"* or *"I won an award."* Indicate positive things you did to help your organizations. Describe how you helped your management team meet their goals, and also the results they achieved. You can also show how you demonstrated a skill or a personal quality.

Create stories that demonstrate benefits you can bring. If you successfully managed the integration of two teams following a merger, and the new business gained market share and/or costs were reduced—by all means say so. Wherever possible, quantify with dollar amounts, percentages, etc.

Here are some examples of SOAR stories

- **Situation / Opportunity:** When I joined MBC Sales, the company had lost nearly $7.5 million on a new product release. I recognized an opportunity to employ my Procter & Gamble experience in marketing.

- **Action:** With the help of the Y & R agency, I relaunched the brand, created a new television advertising campaign, and refocused all marketing efforts.

- **Result:** Within a year, we turned an $8 million loss to a $4 million gain—30% of the firm's profits.

- **Situation / Opportunity:** The company recruited 5,000 people a year but never had a training program.
- **Action:** I created the firm's first national training course. With a staff of 20, we introduced it in 57 markets.
- **Result:** For the first time, the firm was able to bring in recruits who produced within four weeks. In the following year, sales by newcomers accounted for $3,000,000.

You'll also need to neutralize employer perceptions about your liabilities.

Everyone who recruits is on the lookout for liabilities, reasons to rule you out... not in. Listed below are the results of a survey we did of 2,500 professionals who were still in the job market *after a period of 12 months.* The percentages relate to what they felt were the reasons for their problems.

Search issues they blamed their problems on

96%+	Lacked access to right openings
91%+	Needed better resume
87%+	Lacked industry options
77%+	Failed in interviews

Liability issues they blamed their problems on

68%+	Unemployment hurt
65%+	Age was a problem
62%+	Too specialized
55%+	Experience in a single industry
47%+	Lacked blue chip experience
29%+	Changed jobs too often
22%+	Titles lacked career progression
20%+	Previous firm performed poorly
20%+	Reference issues
16%+	Left short term job
15%+	Recent jobs were too similar
13%+	Had shifted from main field
9%+	Was seen as overqualified

The liability issues can come back to haunt you. If you plan how you will neutralize them, you will save yourself from an enormous amount of anxiety and keep from drifting in the market. Any good marketer, whether it's Dell Computer, Honda or IBM... knows their products aren't perfect, but they find ways to market them and overcome any shortcomings!

This section listed the skills and experience factors that employers want. The most important ones that apply to you should be used in all job hunting communications.

How McKenzie Scott helps with rule #3
Expand your marketability... far
beyond your factual credentials

We pinpoint the vital phrases that should be used consistently in all your communications, and which will expand your marketability. We also help you develop your best 8 to 10 "SOAR stories." Our Marketing Directors use them in your written materials, and you use them in your telephone and interview discussions. We also suggest ways for best neutralizing any liabilities that might restrict your search.

RULE #4

Pursue New Industry Options
And Focus On Growth Situations.

Pinpoint your best new industry options... consider growth industries and smaller firms... not just large employers.

Today, people must be prepared to market themselves with sufficient skill so that they are attractive to employers across a broad range. The reality is that people of all ages are making moves into emerging industries. Many find such choices allow them to have greater income and more challenge. Here, we'll share some basics we've learned.

Transition to a new industry is easier than it used to be. Historically, people have overrated the barriers and underrated their abilities to move into new areas.

Today, the vast majority of all new jobs are created by small and mid-sized business units. So, while major employers are still important, you may want to explore positions with start-ups or emerging companies. Here is a quick summary of why it's so important for people to choose the right industry.

If you choose the right industry, you will have more growth opportunities, perhaps meaningful stock options, an environment that is likely to be more positive, a chance for more regular pay increases and probably a longer term career.

How to identify your new industry options

The first way is to identify the fastest growing industries and companies. These firms go outside their industry to find the best talent and skills. Previous industry experience is secondary. The second way is to list characteristics of your industries... and then find similar industries. We have software which compares your industry's characteristics with 2500 others... e.g. 35 industries may be an 85% match.

As a rule, when we work with a client we identify a range of possibilities that people may not have uncovered on their own. Keep in mind that projecting some form of an industry hook is the next best thing to having industry experience. When we compile a person's best possibilities, we often group them three ways:

1. *close industry hooks... easy possibilities;*
2. *medium industry hooks... next best;*
3. *far reach or stretch industry hooks.*

The more you know about an industry, the easier it is to get interviews. Conversely, the harder it is to demonstrate industry awareness, the less likely you will move into it.

If you are short on information about an industry, one way to acquire knowledge is by speaking with people in the industry or through trade publications. They make it easy to talk about new products, specific firms and the major industry challenges. Our software can also be used to supply you with a wealth of knowledge.

Executives who have worked for firms under pressure can be invaluable contributors. Tough lessons learned in competitive battles can put you in demand in new industries. Also, while glamorous high-tech and service businesses receive 90% of all publicity, many people will find far more opportunities in industries that are considered low-tech... or which have problems.

When changing industries, you also don't want to overlook your leverage power... the added benefits you may bring by virtue of your contacts or knowledge. You may be able to bring a team with you that helped you "turn around" a similar situation. Perhaps you control major accounts. Or, you may have cut costs and can do it again.

When you identify your industry options... and market your transferable skills... you expand your market by 300% to 500%. This is the key to changing industries... and without strain or worry.

**How McKenzie Scott helps with rule #4
Pursue new industry options
and focus on growth situations**

We use our file of faster growing firms to isolate certain growth industries—where your skills are likely to be more important than prior industry experience. Then, from thousands of other industries, we use software to isolate industries with "similar characteristics"—to those in which you have had prior experience—situations you might wish to explore.

RULE #5

Use A Multiple Resume Concept
For Greater Immediate Response.

You can get much greater "awareness" by using several different resumes—and by adjusting your approach to the market's new rules for resume success.

Unfortunately, when we look for a job, we're reduced to how we look on paper. 95% of resumes are inadequate. They are average in appearance, disclose liabilities and are rarely about what people can contribute.

Since the early 1990s, the growth in the use of PCs, fax machines, the Internet and email has resulted in firms receiving *50 times* more resumes than in the past. Many employers have also embraced resume-scanning software and shifted to new ways of selection.

In this environment, McKenzie Scott, as a result of tracking thousands of searches, has developed a more effective approach—one which utilizes several types of resumes, all targeted for different applications. The edge this can provide is significant.

We feel that resumes must package all your key skills and experiences that are relevant to your goals. The style, tone and every word must be crafted to capture the best expression of what you have to offer. When you have an "A" resume it's not likely to be just two times more effective than a "B" resume—*it's more likely to be 100 times more effective.*

To succeed in less time, chances are you will have to abandon your old ideas about resumes… and 95% of what everyone accepts as conventional wisdom. These pages will share what we have learned.

To generate activity... a resume that makes your phone ring must meet these 7 criteria

■ The resume should ideally be one page in length.

■ At the top, list the jobs you want.

■ Your resume must be scanning-ready with key words related to the jobs you want—under your goals.

■ The 1st third of your resume must be a summary.

■ Your resume must avoid revealing any liabilities.

■ Your resume must sell transferable skills.

■ It must present a first class image.

Your universal resume

The most essential resume you need is a universal resume—a one-page document that will be your introductory resume. It is the first resume we do for all of our clients.

Most people mistakenly believe that they need to tell their whole story in their initial resume. The reality is that you get better results when your initial resume is interesting, with a feeling of action—but short! This resume must be suitable for key word scanning, with short paragraphs, and be easy to read and compelling. From a content standpoint, it must be headlined by a simple job title listing (e.g. Director of Marketing) that an employer might have available.

Your electronic or "Internet" resume

This is the second resume we do for all clients. It is surprising how few devote any thought to the way their resumes appear at the receiving end of an email transmission. This resume needs to be shorter and to the point... usually no more than two-thirds of one page. When you are online, less is more. All you want is a response.

Your "quick-response" resume

This is the third resume we do for all clients. It's a resume that makes it easy for you to respond quickly to certain emerging situations you discover. This resume positions the text on the right-hand side of the page so that you can write handwritten notes and dispatch a resume without a cover letter. Clients consistently tell us that executives respond well to their notes which cited events that were signals of emerging jobs.

Your "interview" resume

An interview resume is designed to be a persuasive summary which intentionally reveals more about you. It is for presenting during or after your interviews when it is clear that employers want to know more about you. Since it reveals more about your industry experiences, it could hurt your response if used as an introductory resume. However, once you've been interviewed this detailed summary can be a more compelling sales document.

Your C-Level biography

Originally called a "bio-narrative" resume, the C-Level biography can be extremely powerful. It is essential for those competing for a CEO or COO job, or who expect to be hired with the approval of the president or CEO. As a rule, anyone seeking $200,000 or more should have this document. Decision makers at this level often pass on a resume to get consensus. The offer depends on a "thumbs up" from the resume presentation. A three to five page resume, it is written in a narrative style and from a third-party perspective. It uses long stories, rich in detail, and is favored by top recruiters because it makes their jobs easier.

McKenzie Scott clients on resumes

■ *"Adjectives would not adequately convey my admiration for your C-Level biography concept."*

■ *"Having a variety of truly customized written materials expanded my potential by a very significant level."*

■ *"I had a string of unavoidable short term experiences. The communication of these experiences, in narrative form, and how my age was handled, made all the difference."*

Use customized marketing letters— a neglected concept in job hunting

Use customized letters… tailored to the needs of organizations, and you will start generating far more interviews for high quality situations. Letters can sometimes be more important than resumes. But, you must customize your appeal to each audience. The letters people normally require can include the following 12 letters for different occasions:

- For responding to openings
- For contacting recruiters
- For contacting venture capitalists
- For responding to spot opportunities
- For direct mail contact with employers
- For sponsored direct mail to employers
- For contacting directors of associations
- For networking associates and friends
- For networking alumni from your university
- For networking influential people
- For setting up potential references
- For following up your interviews

Cover letters you use should be interesting and brief. Get to the point and make sure it's good.

Letter resumes are stand-alone letters that you will forward without a resume. They are suggested when you want to tailor the description of your credentials and avoid revealing any liabilities. They are recommended for people changing careers or industries.

Handwritten memos are fast and easy to send off, plus executives are used to them. If you have a superior resume that is on target for your audience, attaching such notes can work very well. Obviously, the content of all your letters will be critically important. Materials that emphasize what you can do, as well as the results you can bring, are ideal.

Before writing your letters, have a clear picture of what you want to say. To avoid being disorganized, the opening should demonstrate your interest (knowledge of the firm, its industry, etc.) and explain your reason for writing. The body should deal with your best selling points and convey benefits. Then enlarge upon your selling points, citing related achievements. The closing should restate your interest, confirm your desire for an interview, and say when you will followup. Keep it simple. These letters are usually skimmed, not analyzed.

McKenzie Scott's 20 basic letter writing guidelines

1   Use the name of the person or firm in the letter.
2   Letters are warmer if you use pronouns such as "I" or "we."
3   Good letters are fast moving. They read like you speak.
4   Always be enthusiastic about your subject.
5   If you have related industry experience, mention it early.
6   Communicate potential benefits if possible.
7   Keep sentences short and paragraphs to five or six lines.
8   Don't oversell. "If this guy is so good, why the hard sell?"
9   Never begin a letter by asking for a job.
10   When answering ads, tailor response to the requirements.
11   When possible, offer to share some beneficial "ideas."
12   Avoid income and don't explain why you are looking.
13   Use action words and direct brief descriptions.
14   Sign letters with your full name (never initials).
15   Edit your letters and read them out loud. If you lose your breath, the sentences are too long.
16   Commit yourself to a follow-up at a date and time.
17   When writing to employers who have been undergoing change, cite the opportunities implied by your information that relate to your experience.
18   If you are addressing an influential person, recognize their position in a complimentary manner and be brief.
19   Having a third party send your letters can be powerful. Their statements can act as a strong endorsement. You don't have to be a close friend to ask for third party assistance. Just make it easy for the third party to assist. Offer to prepare a letter for their signature.
20   Follow-up letters must show continued enthusiasm.

Using a multiple resume concept will immediately lift your response level by 100% to 200%... or more!

How McKenzie Scott helps with rule #5
Use a multiple resume concept
for greater immediate response

Our staff professionally writes your universal, electronic and quick response resumes. Our goal is to capture the best expression of your experiences and skills plus your ability to contribute at the next level. We can also professionally draft all of the marketing letters you might require. On an optional basis for many people, we can develop a superior interview resume or C-Level biography to assist in your search.

RULE #6

Multiply The Openings You Uncover
By A Minimum of 10 Times.

Thanks to the Internet, all published openings can now be at your fingertips. Here's how to respond to them.

We recommend that you gain exposure to as many advertised openings as possible and that you tailor your message to the requirements of most advertisements.

One way to increase your number of opportunities is to understand the process of upgrading or downgrading ads. For example, a company advertising a Vice President position may be willing to hire an Assistant Vice President or Director, who could move up to Vice President within a year. After all, it isn't so much the title they are after as the skills and talent. That's an example of ***downgrading.***

By the same token, a firm advertising for a Plant Manager might be persuaded to hire a VP of Manufacturing, provided someone could persuade them such a move would be cost efficient and give added capabilities. That's an ***upgrade.***

In addition to downgrading and upgrading, advertised openings can also be used as signals of private openings in other areas of the company. This is called ***sidegrading.***

If, for instance, you see a company hiring a number of salespeople, that's a fairly reliable indicator that they are also hiring people in sales administration, production and other areas. This approach can be very effective for people at lower levels who see openings for senior level positions in their field. It is important to write to the "functional chief" when upgrading, downgrading or sidegrading. HR will typically be the last to know of an emerging job (except in HR).

Did you ever see an ad and feel "that describes me exactly"? Well, as a general rule, you should follow up on every ad for which you are well qualified. Very few of your competitors will do this. At the very least, it will improve your odds for getting your credentials looked at.

You should also keep in mind that using letters alone and following up can help your response rate. Employers who must sift through many resumes tend to start by screening out non-qualifiers. And, since resumes provide more facts, they can sometimes work against you. For this reason, when answering ads of special interest, use a strong letter tailored to the requirements of the position.

Sometimes a handwritten note attached to your resume can be effective. This is advisable when there are relatively few points you wish to communicate. For example, when an employer has a few key requirements, and they can be restated in a short note to reinforce your qualifications.

Employers rarely find the perfect candidate. So, try to compensate for any shortfall on credentials through an expression of enthusiasm, or by explaining why you might be particularly well qualified for other reasons. Whatever your basis for selecting an advertisement, let the employer know why you selected it.

Creative response approaches

A number of people have had success using the following approaches:

■ One is to get additional information, beyond what was in the ad, and use it in your response. This can be achieved by reviewing product literature, websites, annual reports, or newspaper articles. Demonstrating industry knowledge works better than anything else.

■ Another technique is to develop third party contacts with employees in the company before responding. Easiest to befriend are sales and marketing managers, public relations staffers, or top level executives. Then, you can consider mentioning their names in your correspondence.

Privacy issues and the Internet

Once your resume is posted on any number of major Internet job boards, you have no idea of the people who may have access to viewing your material. Almost all major job boards make use of some form of resume scanning software. They sell access to their database of resumes to employers looking for candidates. Since every word in your resume is scannable, someone who uses their services might uncover your resume. This is just one more reason for using short resumes, materials that don't reveal anything unnecessary... on the Internet. Some of the major job boards include the following:

6-Figure Jobs	Chief Monster	Hot Jobs
America's Job Bank	CIO.com	Job Bank USA
Career Builder	DICE.com	Jobs.com
Career Exchange	Direct Employers	Monster
Career Magazine	Direct-Jobs.com	Nationjobs
CareerJournal.com	FlipDog.com	Net-temps
CFO.com		

Until recently, it was never possible, but you can now uncover virtually the entire published market... and see just what's out there for you.

How McKenzie Scott helps with rule #6 Multiply the openings you uncover by a minimum of ten times

With our Job Market Access Center, you have instant access to approximately 1,700,000 openings. You simply click on boxes like those shown below. The company also provides its own special software... called "advertised market supersearch" which allows you to expedite frequent searches. This software searches several hundred newspapers and job boards simultaneously—for a specific job title of interest.

2,100	3,500	300	3,500	100,000
Newspapers	Trade Mag's	Job Boards	Recruiters	Employers

RULE #7

Market Yourself To Several
Thousand Recruiters—Simultaneously.

Giving your credentials exposure to a maximum number of recruiters should be mandatory for most people.

Whether they are called search firms or headhunters, all recruiters work for employers. Their function is to locate, screen and recommend prospective employees. These firms *are not* in business to serve job hunters. They fill jobs at $60,000 to $1,000,000 and up. Typically, they are retained for exclusive searches at fees averaging up to 33% of compensation.

To distinguish themselves, executive search firms are referred to as "retained recruiters." Other firms, called contingency recruiters, are active up to $150,000, but receive a commission only when a placement is made.

Another growing category is the "temporary or contract recruiter." They earn fees when employers hire professionals on an interim basis. The number of jobs with recruiters is sizeable, and comprises about 7% to 9% of the market. While 8,000 firms claim to be active, fewer than 30 dominate the upper-end business. Importantly, the best recruiters play a role in helping management set up position specifications.

Local and regional recruiters have been playing an increasingly important role in the job market. Some specialize by industry... and others by career fields. Today, there are thousands of local recruiters which can be helpful.

Recruiters are articulate professionals who have a broad knowledge of business, and who are excellent marketing executives themselves. It will pay you to develop relationships with those you respect and to maintain them throughout your career. They know what's going on in their local markets.

Recruiters prefer achievers, people making strong first impressions and who are employed. Being visible in your industry can be key. Being in a hot field or industry can really help. Of course, to develop any level of good activity with recruiters, you'll need superior materials.

When you communicate with recruiters, never be negative about your employer and never appear desperate. Also, keep in mind that recruiters are "assignment-oriented." They need to fill their active contracts or job listings. So, when you send them a resume, or register online, most of the time your resume will simply be placed in their files.

What to expect from resume distributions to recruiters

■ People with recognizable "tickets" do best (for example, well-known schools, degrees, blue chip affiliations, etc.).

■ People in popular occupations also do best. Some response is immediate, but most come in over months.

■ Contacting recruiters is less effective for those in low demand specialties or for those making a career change.

■ Also, as you go up the pyramid, since fewer jobs are available, the response will be lower. Overall, it's a low percentage game. That is why you need greater numbers.

■ A second distribution to the same list three to four months later produces about 80% of the initial response.

When responses come in and they engage you on the phone, be ready with your 30-second or 60-second commercial. Also, keep in mind that you will be most popular with recruiters if you will explore attractive situations, but are not openly unhappy. Because timing is critical, luck can also play a role.

Remember that the chance of a recruiter filling a job that is right for you, at the moment you contact them is small.

That's why contacting a lot of recruiters must be an essential part of any search.

How McKenzie Scott helps with rule #7
Market yourself to several
thousand recruiters simultaneously

We can market you to up to 200 local recruiters. And, we can market you to approximately 3,000 national recruiters who have asked to receive the resumes of our clients. As an option, we can also market you to 1,000 premier recruiters who scan resumes.

A surprising number of VC firms have assumed an active role in recruiting for firms in which they have an ongoing investment. People who will generate the most interest are executives who are candidates for "C" level positions (COO, CTO, etc.) or those who can fill a role as head of a line function (VP Sales, etc.). Typically, they are in their 30s and 40s, have been with major firms and have advanced degrees.

Through our Job Market Access Center, you can also review openings that thousands of recruiters post online. If your background is appropriate, our Marketing Directors will also market you to local venture capitalists.

RULE #8

Contact Employers Directly With
A Direct Mail Concept That Works.

Targeted custom direct mail... especially to growth or change-driven firms—can be a fast way to find the right new job.

You have probably seen ads for mailing services with strong success claims. Unfortunately, many executives have purchased such services, sending out up to 15,000 mailings, with no results! These services don't work, because the firms send out five-line cover letters attached to historical resumes. They simply don't qualify people for new industries.

On the other hand... if carefully targeted at decision makers in industries for which your materials have built a strong candidacy, direct mail can be very productive.

Why does direct mail work? Every day we all receive direct mail. However bad that junk mail looks, the ones you see again and again are working; otherwise, the senders wouldn't be wasting money repeating the process.

Historically, a primary rule in direct mail is that long copy is the name of the game. That's what it takes to motivate all of us to action from *unasked-for correspondence*.

Here's an example. Let's say your local lawn mower shop wants you to come in and see a new product they're carrying. And you and your next door neighbor are both out cutting your lawns on a hot day. However, your lawn mower keeps stopping, and finally breaks down.

Then, the mail carrier arrives at both residences with mail that tells you all about a new lawn mower. It gives a long explanation of why it's superior to everything. Now, chances are your neighbor will look at the mailing piece for two seconds and toss it, wondering how anyone could ever read all the material. Obviously, he isn't in the market for a lawn mower. On the other hand, because the mailing piece has reached you at the right time, you are apt to read it carefully, and perhaps make a purchase!

Now, your position, relative to using direct mail, is really quite similar. Your interest is in reaching the right person who might be in the market for someone like you right now. No one else counts.

I asked a friend of mine, a CEO of a high tech company, what he thought of direct mail. His response was, *"Well, I get a lot of resumes and even some from my board members who pass on candidates that look good. It works if the person really comes across well."*

Another friend, a VP of Marketing at a Fortune 500 company, put it another way. He said, *"I look at resumes that cross my desk. If something matches my needs at the moment, I usually respond directly. It's a matter of timing."*

How some McKenzie Scott clients view direct mail

■ *"I focused on firms in three metro areas.... Dallas, Houston, and Denver. In 8 weeks I had 12 viable situations develop and two turned into good offers."*

■ *"We did major mailings in foods and pharmaceuticals. Results continued for months. My new position is a divisional COO for Pfizer."*

■ *"Highly targeted third-party mailings were critical. They went out under the names of close friends and the response was excellent."*

A third associate, the head of HR at a Fortune 500 company, sent me the following when I was updating this book. His comment was, *"I would highly recommend direct mail. Third-party letters can be especially effective if the right person is writing for you. Just prepare a letter they approve for their signature. Make it easy for them to assist."*

Compile your mailing list with each person's correct title, spelling of their name and address. Since most reference sources are 15-20% out-of-date *(including the best)*, if it is an important target, call for correct information.

Now, you must recognize that a very low percentage of employers will need someone like you the day your material arrives. For example, take a CFO position. *These jobs turn over only once every three years.* This means the week your mailing arrives might be perfect... but only once in every 156 weeks, if it gets to the right person. For executives, from 3 to 6 positive responses, sometimes up to 10, typically are generated from 1,000 mailings. Obviously, your success will depend on a host of personal and market factors at the time. Of course, if you had five very good situations to explore, you might not need anything else.

Unlike responding to openings or contacting recruiters, direct mail often produces highly qualified leads in a non-competitive situation. After all, they will have read about you, and want to see you for what your material represents. They will either have a position... or they may be thinking about creating a position.

A key point to remember is that when responses are received, you need to make the most of them. Other than a brief discussion, never be interviewed on the phone and never rule anything out. You can always use the responses to upgrade within the same firm or to network.

Selecting your mailing list

Let's review our principles that have helped make direct mail successful for other clients. First of all, your objective is to reach the right person... who might be in the market for your talents—right now. No one else counts. As you approach selecting a mailing list, you want to compile a list of your highest probability targets. Take into consideration your industry and location preferences.

For senior executives, we suggest focusing on the CEO or board members of firms in target industries. Now, in a very large firm, you may be unsure whom to contact. People with varying titles, for example... Group VP, North American Operations, may be running several divisions or business units.

If possible, do some research to identify the specific decision maker who would be most interested in your message. As an alternative, it can sometimes be appropriate to make contact

Classify your mailing list. 10% should be viewed as your "best-of-best" possibilities... worthy of follow-up and repeat mailings. Another 20% should be considered "primary" possibilities; and the balance would be "secondary" possibilities.

with the CFO. He or she may be aware of opportunities across many operations... and may have the ear of the CEO.

Direct mail response is best for smaller and mid-sized firms. In the larger organizations which interest you, you will want to **consider multiple mailings to different executives.** In one case, approaching an employer with 28,000 employees in one metro area, each week, for 12 weeks, we mailed to a decision maker in the firm—until an interview in the area we wanted was secured.

In smaller firms, target owners or top officers. They can be decisive and make hiring decisions more quickly. Follow-up mailings after 90 days will generally produce 80% of the response of your original mailing.

Contacting board members is worth some separate comment. When you do this, it has to be done with dignity. Our approach is to send out custom letters under our letterhead each week. For each contact, we include a custom cover letter with the universal resume and a C-Level biography. This lets board members have a thumbnail sketch and an extensive recitation of your credentials and abilities in their C-Level biography. This presentation is similar to a board briefing book that a member would receive prior to a board meeting.

The types of direct mail actions that work best

Let's assume you were a district sales manager seeking a national sales manager's job. Here is a range of direct mail actions you might consider taking.

- **Most Popular.** Sent to CEOs. Takes good credentials in mainstream fields to work. Response will be low from large firms, but better from smaller/ mid-sized companies.

- **Much Better.** Sent to SVP sales by personal name, selected by industry, size and location. Can be very good with follow-up to your "best-of-best" prospects.

- **Excellent.** Sent to SVP sales to whom you have spoken. Or, sent to SVP Sales, by name, where a third party mailing goes out under someone else's letterhead.

- **Outstanding.** Sent to SVP sales, by name, to whom you've been referred or met or spoken to via phone.

- **Often Best.** Continuous direct mail to penetrate organizations which are your high probability prospects… your best of best. For example, if you get no interest from a first mailing, proceed to contact a minimum of five other decision makers in mid-sized firms (300 to 1,000) and up to 12 in large organizations or divisions—spaced out over eight weeks (with phone follow up).

Custom mailings to 1,000, 3,000 or 5,000 targets are often essential

The vast majority of all professionals and executives should do custom direct mail to employers at a level of 1,000 to 3,000… and some to 5,000. Many executives we serve have traditionally done mailings to several thousand employers. Naturally, each case is individual. For people interested in regional or national campaigns, as well as those who are marketable across many industries, this level of aggressiveness is essential.

Cover letters attached to the universal resume are recommended for most situations. However, handwritten notes on a quick response resume can also be effective.

Essential for most people seeking above $150K, marketing by direct mail requires a sophisticated effort. Superior materials, the right targets and timing all play a key role.

**How McKenzie Scott helps with rule #8
Contact employers directly with
a direct mail concept that works**

We market you thru direct mail to local growth firms, key employers, recruiters and VCs. We can process major custom mailings, both locally and nationally, to 1,000 to 5,000 officers and board members or VCs nationwide. You can also do your own direct mail with the materials we prepare... using lists obtained from our Job Market Access Center.

RULE #9

Use "Breaking News" To
Connect With Emerging Jobs.

**News releases can alert you to emerging situations...
jobs that are not yet competitive. Jobs can also be created
when you present yourself as a solution to a problem
or opportunity—as signaled by a news event.**

Every day, events occur in tens of thousands of firms that
lead decision makers to begin the process of privately looking
for new people. These events are often reported in local and
national business publications, trade magazines, newsletters
and newspapers. They are essentially signals of emerging
jobs... and that hiring will soon follow.

What kinds of news events signal emerging jobs?

- News of an employer receiving new capital
- A firm kicking off a new product introduction
- Announcements of executive appointments
- Word of new local business operations
- New contracts being awarded
- News of planned relocations by employers
- Major licensing agreements being announced
- Announcements of expectations of growth
- Announcements of record annual profits

For companies undergoing these transitions, chances are
they will need to attract good people to handle problems or
capitalize on their opportunities. Their activities won't just be
limited to one or two functions. They can be expected to need
people in all functional categories: sales, marketing, finance,
etc. What's more, when you connect with these situations,
they will generally be much less competitive than you will
experience when competing for published openings.

How The Job
Market Is Formed

Events occur
- Firms get capital
- New businesses are started
- Major contracts are awarded
- Record profits lead to expansion
- Current staff leave or retire
- New products are created
- Firms relocate

Jobs are planned for
These events cause executives to think about hiring new staff.

As jobs are released and decisions are made... the job market is formed

Jobs become available in one of these segments

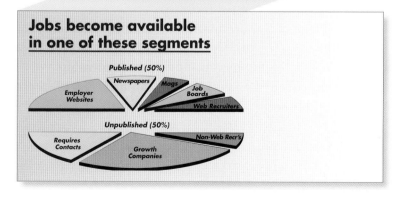

Don't ignore firms
with problems

Reorganizations involve shifts within the executive ranks. They usually spell opportunity for those who are at the next lower level, and then changes ripple through the organization down the line.

Problems often imply one of two things: managers in certain functions haven't been performing well, or the company needs to develop new capabilities in order to survive and grow. Organizations with problems often need help from the following types of people:

- Marketing people who can identify new markets and find new applications for existing products.

- Sales people who can increase volume.

- Applications engineers who can design new products and applications for existing products.

- Financial staff who can cut costs or raise capital.

- Manufacturing people who can find more cost efficient ways to produce goods and reduce overhead.

- Skilled negotiators who can win more favorable terms with labor and suppliers.

- Real estate and financial people who can redeploy assets or dispose of unwanted facilities.

- General managers who can take total responsibility for plant closings, consolidations and streamlinings.

- CEOs and COOs who can supply new leadership.

- Human resource executives who can help find all these people, while directing outplacement activities with certain parts of the work force.

How some McKenzie Scott clients
made the breaking news strategy work

▪ *"I read that a troubled manufacturer was divesting a division to raise cash. I called the new president. Four weeks later, I became CFO."*

▪ *"I was a product manager. Seeing that a local firm had been acquired, I sent a letter to express interest. 12 weeks later, I became VP Marketing, U.S.A."*

▪ *"My previous job was as a GM. I read that a major investment was being made near my home. I got through after three attempts to the CEO and in one month was offered a position."*

▪ *"I was an administrator of a university hospital. I read about a medical equipment firm and soon started in a position with 20% higher income."*

▪ *"I had been in sales and wanted to run U.S. marketing for a Japanese photocopier manufacturer. An article from your breaking news program led me to the job I wanted."*

▪ *"I read about the training challenges of a local software company. Inside of three weeks I was able to move from my long term career field of education to a firm with a lot of growth opportunity."*

Don't miss opportunities
to get a job created for you

You can develop offers, even when no current openings exist. You simply need to present yourself as a solution to a problem. In fact, the higher you go, the more likely your next position will be created for you, or at least reshaped to fit your talents.

The organizations most likely to create a job will include firms that are growing rapidly, bringing out new products, forming new divisions, acquiring other companies, or reorganizing. These are the firms that need good people, often from other industries, who make decisions quickly.

Your goal would be to communicate directly with the person you would most likely work for, or their boss. The key for you is to be able to communicate a suitable benefit proposition. This should be a concise description of what you can do. You need to present the promise of value on a scale large enough to warrant an investment in you. In your initial communication, you must establish your credentials and mention past results. Achievements you cite don't have to be large, but they do have to be significant.

Dealing with opportunities is a key job for many executives. Most don't have enough time, and they are predisposed to positive news from people who can help them. They will want to believe your message.

Remember, when you go to the interview, you're going to have to address the benefits that your communication promised. You can expect questions such as: *What are your ideas? What makes you confident that they'll work? Do you really understand this company, its problems and its opportunities?* Address these areas, but always remember to convey humility. Acknowledge that the other person has a better grasp of the problems than you could possibly have.

One of your first goals is to find out how the employer views the problem. *What do they see as the key challenges? What is their "hot button"? Where are their priorities? What attempts have been made in the past?*

By asking a few questions and listening carefully, you will find out what the employer really wants. Ask questions and make positive comments in response to the interviewer's remarks. Try to get the employer to share his innermost thoughts—his vision for the firm. If you are able to accomplish this in the first interview, that's enough.

In your second interview, reinforce your value by drawing a picture of the benefits you can bring. Then, build enough enthusiasm to get an offer or be asked to speak with others.

Keep in mind that you will need to stir the employer's imagination. Your conversations should focus on the future. Convey enthusiasm and create a sense of excitement. Be ready to discuss approaches you would take to reinforce the notion that you will succeed. If you build sufficient enthusiasm, the employer may conclude the meeting with a statement that they want to create a job for you.

Using "breaking news" to find emerging opportunities ... is the most underutilized ... and perhaps most highly effective way... to find and compete for unpublished jobs.

How McKenzie Scott helps with rule #9
Use "breaking news" to
connect with emerging jobs

Our Marketing Directors set "search agents" for you to automatically deliver relevant news stories... as soon as they break. This enormously valuable information is a major key to allowing you to compete in the unpublished job market. You can then use our letters or our quick response resume to respond to situations. The same news can be used to contact firms who may be candidates to create a job for you.

RULE #10

Network By Using Excellent Letters
And Pursue An Industry Focus.

Dismiss your old ideas about networking. Pursue "industry targeted" approaches which save time.

Networking, is a pyramiding strategy... one where you capitalize on one name to gain an interview with another. We recommend that you focus your networking on industries which have characteristics that make you a good match.

Seeking *informational interviews* is the most popular networking approach. Here, you wish to encourage executives to share with you some information about their industry, trends and challenges, and so on.

These discussions must be kept brief, and you need to have your list of questions prepared. As a rule, executives do better when they have researched a firm and ask for feedback on ideas that may benefit the firm.

Executives to target should be influential people. Consider looking for those who have been featured or quoted in articles, which makes an introduction easy and natural. Also be sure to track down lost contacts, uncover successful alumni and others. Executive Directors of associations have many "lines" into their industries. Editors of business magazines and newsletters may also have an inside track on the needs of specific organizations.

We all have influential friends... golfing partners, politicians, lawyers, investment bankers, etc., who know others who could be looking for someone like you. All they need to do is handwrite a short note and forward your materials.

Networking through references

Mark was a VP who wanted to become a CFO. We helped make Mark aware of the power of his references. When Mark heard his company was to be sold, he felt his salary was $20,000 less than it should be.

Did his boss feel bad about paying him less than he was worth? Absolutely! Could Mark ask him to act as a reference, and would he raise him to the level he wanted, in return for staying for the last two months? Definitely.

Now, the boss had a friend in an accounting firm. Mark asked his boss if he would approach his friend as a second reference. Together, they had lunch. The accountant was happy to be a second reference. In the same way, Mark developed a third reference, his own brother-in-law.

When he launched a campaign, he had a good interview with the president of a small paper company. A conservative man, he asked for three references. Mark immediately recontacted his references, so they were ready. After his boss had given him a glowing reference, the president mentioned that he was still uncertain.

When the second reference was called (the boss's friend), he told the president that in the right situation Mark could help save $1 million in taxes, and control costs. He had repositioned Mark as a broader-based financial executive.

Next, Mark's third reference supported the others and added a few points. The day after the last reference check, he got a call from the president, and guess what? His message was, *"Mark, what will it take to get you?"* He ended up as CFO at a much higher income.

Most of the time, important references will be the people you reported to in the past, or the person you currently report to or their superiors. Choose the highest level reference, as long as you get an enthusiastic endorsement, and avoid people who don't communicate well. Also be sure to give them an idea of what to emphasize about your background.

Selecting your references

References you select should know your achievements and have no hesitation in making strong statements. What they say is very important, but the enthusiasm and conviction they project is more important. Let them know that you have high regard for them and their opinions, and they will want to do their very best.

Also, make sure that your references know the full story. Here's an example. A woman who worked for me left to complete her MBA. She was competent, had a quiet manner, but could be forceful. When she started interviewing, she brought me up-to-date. She called after an interview to tell me that she felt they had some concerns about her quiet nature. Armed with that information, I was ready when I was called by her potential boss. Before the question was asked, I mentioned that sometimes people could be deceived by this woman's quiet nature, but that she could be very assertive. The person responded that I had put to rest his one concern.

A sample networking letter to an "influential person"... and sharing your biography

Dear Mr. Kearns:

As President of Mellon Bank and a person well known in financial circles, you have insight into many firms. That is the reason for this letter.

My most recent executive assignment has been as CFO of Carter Inc. In that position, my achievements contributed heavily to the following results:

- *A major profit decline was reversed as our earnings have jumped 30% within two years.*

- *A complete reorganization was put into effect and a new EDP system was successfully installed.*

Earlier, I held increasingly responsible positions with Henredon, a manufacturer of quality furniture.

Now, after careful thought, I have decided to seek out new opportunities in Pittsburgh. I know you are busy, but thought perhaps you could share my background with an associate who could benefit from my experience. CEOs or board members of consumer product manufacturers would be logical possibilities.

With this in mind, I am taking the liberty of enclosing a few biographies. Thank you in advance for your help. I will call your secretary next week to see if you might wish any further information.

With best regards,

Thomas Singleton

Thomas Singleton

References can be your best sources of referrals. Leave each person a half-dozen resumes. Reassure them that you won't use them too many times. After calling them, send a brief note that shows your appreciation and summarize a few positive things they can say about you. You can even make a list of questions that employers might ask and suggest answers for them.

By the way, let references know as soon as you have used their names, and ask them to let you know when they have been contacted. Employers will sometimes ask them for the name of someone else who is familiar with you.

Questionable references

If someone is apt to give you a bad reference, you need to bring it out in the interview and supply enough good ones to offset it.

For example, if the interviewer asks to speak with a reference who will be questionable, defuse the situation by explaining that you had differences of opinion on some managerial styles. Remain totally objective and unemotional, and never imply negatives about that person.

Also, if you are doubtful about what a reference might say, you might have a friend do a mock reference check to find out what is being said. If the reference is neutral, don't hesitate to ask the person to furnish more positive information. If necessary, explain that any negative input is keeping you from winning a position and enabling you to support yourself and your family. As a last resort, you may have to imply that you will seek a legal remedy.

One of the major keys to effective networking rests with your ability to create superior "networking letters." Some examples in this section will give you the idea.

A sample networking letter to an "old friend"... and sharing your biography

Dear Sherrill,

It isn't often, unfortunately, that I write letters to old friends. There's a good reason for doing so now and it involves a favor.

As you may know, I have had a successful consulting practice over recent years. However, I have decided to seek out a new line assignment as president of a small corporation, or as marketing executive with a larger firm.

As part of this new direction, I am interested in expanding my acquaintances at the level of CEO. Considering your long history in the area, it seems that you may be able to provide me with a few select introductions.

Ideal contacts would be with CEOs with firms having significant growth potential. A company facing a turnaround situation could also be interesting.

In any event, I hope to move swiftly in securing appropriate contacts. If you don't mind, I would like to review some possibilities with you... situations which may signal the need for a person like myself.

Please give my best regards to Phil. Thanks in advance for your time. I'll give you a ring later in the week.

With my best regards,

Gordon Edwards

Gordon Edwards

McKenzie Scott's basic guidelines
for executive networking

■ Network only with materials that are just right.

■ List the people you want to see, and find a way to get someone to help you meet them.

■ Know what you want to say, the questions to ask, and the strengths to emphasize.

■ Exchange cards and talk with people wherever you go. Let them know you are thinking about something new.

■ Try to leave every meeting with new names.

■ Remember the names of the front office staff.

■ Send a thank you note after each meeting.

■ People know when they're "being networked." That doesn't mean they won't help, but don't try to fool them.

Traditional networking often takes a long time and some find it demeaning. Networking which utilizes superior letters with an industry focus can be very productive.

How McKenzie Scott helps with rule #10
Network by using excellent letters
and pursue an industry focus

We send your materials to existing contacts that you provide... along with "influential alumni" we identify from your college or university. Through our Job Market Access Center you can uncover old contacts, people you may have lost track of. Our research department will also fulfill any information requests you may have... e.g., for names of executives in targeted industries who may be high probability networking possibilities.

RULE #11

Add Some Telephone Dynamics...
To Power Your Marketing Effort.

Some people resist using the phone as part of their search. But, it can help you achieve far more interviews in a lot less time.

Many of our clients use the phone because they are on the receiving end of substantial interest. Others get on the phone to reach other top executives who can be of help. Effective use of the phone is easier than you think.

If you're not experienced in using the phone, most people are courteous and go out of their way to be helpful. The same holds true for others such as secretaries or assistants.

Still, there is a certain misconception that all assistants will keep you from speaking with their bosses. They do screen calls, but it is part of their job to make sure that contact is made when appropriate. The difference between making phone calls and "teleconnecting" is basic. When you plan to seriously connect, you have specific goals and use a standardized procedure for making a lot of calls.

Approaches for beginning conversations

The good news approach: "*Mr. Ellis, when I heard about your four quarters of growth...*" Here, you build a positive relationship based on specific "good news." Everyone likes to hear from others who are enthusiastic about their good fortune. You can be sure that your message will help to build a feeling of friendliness and warmth over the phone. This kind of approach can play an important role in winning extra interviews and getting people to help you.

The third-party approach: If you mention the name of a third party who knows the person you're calling, it helps to establish rapport, but it's also helpful even when they don't know each other.

"Bill Regan, a partner with McKinsey, thought I should get in touch with you. He felt your growth not only suggests a good investment, but might also indicate a good employment possibility. His insights prompted me to follow up with you personally. Do you have a moment?"

The specific reason approach: Anyone with experience in getting things done can consider this approach.

"Mr. Franklin, I have a 'specific reason' for calling you. I know your line of business and something of the processes you use. During the past 15 months, I have been able to save a company like yours approximately $850,000. I would like to share the details with you. Does your calendar permit a meeting this week?"

The "perhaps-you-can-help-me" approach: *"Hi, Mr. Sands, I'm Tom Cole. Perhaps you can help me. After reading the Fortune article, I wondered if you could refer me to…"*

If an opening has already been filled, someone can help you meet an executive elsewhere in the firm. If the individual you contact does not have a precise fit in his department, perhaps he could help you meet a person in another division. If you are told that the person you want to speak to is out, the best response is, *"Thanks. Perhaps you can help me. When is a good time to call?"*

Handling people
who screen your call

Start by using the name of the person who is the "screener." Once he or she has been identified, their manner will become more personal. When asked your name, identify yourself with an organization if possible. Remember, the more expert the screener is, the more valuable that person can be… as an ally in your future relationships with the firm.

If you don't get through and you can't get a suitable time to call back, suggest a time when you will call back. Until you have established contact, don't leave messages.

When you call back, use the screener's name, and if the person is difficult to reach, try this: "Since he (or she) is so hard to reach, would you do me a small favor? May I call back at one o'clock to see if he would be interested in speaking with me for a few minutes?" If you must leave a message, leave one of potential benefit to the person you are calling.

If the screener refers you to HR, get the name of the person to whom you will be speaking. Call back later for that person or request an immediate transfer. After a few minutes of discussion, ask two or three penetrating questions about the firm's needs. When asked difficult questions, those who don't know the answer are more inclined to refer you to someone.

After a few days, call back the screener and explain that while the HR people were helpful, they couldn't answer the questions you had in mind.

You may encounter the question: "Are you looking for a job?" The answer might be: "Yes I am; do you think you could help me? Though I'm employed, a friend suggested I contact your firm in confidence." Or, you may encounter the comment, "We don't have any openings." The response: "I appreciate a person who is direct; however, I have such a strong interest in the firm, I really believe that with your recent growth, I could be a great asset. May I tell you why?"

McKenzie Scott's key
guidelines for using the phone

■ Get used to making a number of calls at one time. Stand up and you'll give a power assist to your voice.

■ Make sure you know how you will be answering your phone. Don't use clever messages. List questions you may be asked and write out your answers.

■ Prepare a 30-second commercial of your most important selling points. Rehearse it. Critique it.

■ One of the best times to get through to executives is very early in the morning or after 5:00 p.m.

■ Smile while speaking over the phone and your voice will sound more pleasant. Be enthusiastic and positive. When you encounter objections, stay friendly and cooperative, and sometimes answer a question with a question.

■ Project a natural, confident tone... as you would when talking with a friend. Lower your voice. Speak slowly and don't give the impression you're rushed.

■ Be prepared for rejection. Using the phone is a numbers game. You can easily make 15 calls an hour.

■ The screener doesn't know who you are or your purpose. If you retain the thought that you only want advice and information, the decision maker has no reason to shy away from you. When speaking with the secretary, get her name and use it. Be confident, positive, and polite.

■ When following up, do not discuss your business other than to say the executive is expecting your call. Or use your job title to get by the assistant.

■ If you begin to generate interest, don't reveal too much of your story. Remember, you want an interview.

RULE #12

Follow An Action Plan And Expand
Your Market By Up To 30 Times.

Structure your search and you'll be on your way toward getting 85% market exposure... not just the typical 2 to 3%.

Over the years, there have been many occasions when we have seen equally talented executives produce varying results. One will struggle while the other moves with surprising speed and confidence. Those who move with speed usually have had the benefit of a marketing game plan—a step-by-step track to guide their efforts.

In today's competitive arena most people will never get enough interviews with a hit-or-miss approach, or if they depend on one action source. Taking a narrow approach trusts too much to fate.

Think of it this way. Chances are you're marketing a product with millions of dollars of earnings capacity remaining. That much value deserves your best effort. Besides, job hunting is a numbers game. So, why take a chance at doing a lot of things without an aggressive but well-designed plan?

Since job hunting is largely a matter of having the numbers on your side, our action plans are often targeted to produce 15 to 25 positive responses that might lead to interview opportunities. This is necessary because the goal is to have several offers maturing at the same time, and you have to be realistic about rejections.

Our experience is that a good plan can cut job hunting time in half and sometimes save tens of thousands of dollars. It also helps people produce better results, and when people generate a lot of activity in a concentrated time period, they feel better and do better. Much better!

The components of a personal marketing plan

To begin with… (1) you need to pinpoint what you should be marketing—your assets and skills. (2) If you have liabilities you need strategies to neutralize them. (3) You also need to set clear goals and (4) identify the industries to target. (5) You need a step-by-step game plan… the things you'll do to get the right interview activity. Here's a brief recap of what our marketing plans cover.

Assets, transferable skills & how to market them: We will identify your assets and skills and plan how they should be marketed. See our discussion in rule #3… pages 32-43.

Liabilities & solutions: We identify your liability issues, and suggest strategies for minimizing their impact. See page 42.

Job hunting goals: We will recommended appropriate goals… specific job titles to go after in the current job market. To guide your reasoning on this issue, see our discussion relating to pages 20-31.

Industry options: After reviewing fast growing industries and using software to identify industries with characteristics that match your past experience… we target your best industry options. See pages 44-47.

Action plan for getting interviews: We suggest a step-by-step plan to guide your week-by-week activities… a complete game plan… a track for you to follow. It can take advantage of up to 25 ways for getting interviews as described on page 95.

**One of the benefits of
having an action plan is
to avoid job hunting chaos**

Trial and error job hunting can
lead to months of disappointment
and strain, confusion and worry.

Network
a Few
Friends

Answer
Some Ads In
Newspapers

Try Some
Direct Mail
To Ten Large
Companies

Contact
A Few
Recruiters

Network
My Former
Boss

Post My
Resume
On Some
Job Boards

25 ways for getting interviews

We believe in having a weekly goal for interviews you can handle, and gearing your activity to reach this goal. Here is the range of possible actions through all channels into the market.

Respond to openings from these sources weekly

1.	With 2,000 trade magazines	_____ MCKS supplies
2.	With 3,500 newspapers	_____ MCKS supplies
3.	With 300 job boards (e-cruiters)	_____ MCKS supplies
4.	On selected recruiter websites (among 7,500)	_____ MCKS supplies
5.	Among 100,000 employer websites	_____ MCKS supplies
6.	Thru our Advertised Market Supersearch	_____ MCKS supplies

Your credentials are placed with recruiters

7.	With up to 3,000 national recruiters by email	_____ MCKS can do
8.	With up to 200 local firms by 1st class mail	_____ MCKS can do
9.	With 1,000 premier firms which do scanning	_____ MCKS can do

You register your credentials

10.	Register with premier job boards	_____ MCKS supplies
11.	Register with premier recruiters	_____ MCKS supplies

Contacting growth & change-driven firms

12.	Direct mail to local growth firms (up to 200)	_____ MCKS can do
13.	Direct mail to national growth firms (to 1,000)	_____ MCKS can do
14.	Respond to breaking news weekly	_____ MCKS supplies

Following VC investments to opportunities

15.	Search VC investments—leads to openings	_____ MCKS supplies
16.	Place credentials with VCs (to 200)	_____ MCKS can do
17.	Place credentials with VCs (to 1,000)	_____ MCKS can do

Reconnecting with old contacts & new contacts

18.	Exec. to network thru people-finder sites	_____ MCKS supplies
19.	Exec. to network thru search engines	_____ MCKS supplies
20.	Exec. to network thru influential alumni	_____ MCKS supplies
21.	Exec. to network by targeting industries (along with existing friends / acquaintances)	_____ MCKS supplies

Contacting employers & associations directly

22.	Direct mail to key employers (locally to 200)	_____ MCKS can do
23.	Direct mail to U.S. employers (1,000 to 5,000)	_____ MCKS can do
24.	Direct mail to board members if appropriate	_____ MCKS can do
25.	Direct mail to associations	_____ MCKS can do

MCKS = McKenzie Scott

Job hunting is a numbers game. The more contacts you make—the more situations that come your way. An action plan helps keep you on track.

**How McKenzie Scott helps with rule #12
Follow an action plan and expand
your market by up to 30 times**

Our staff will put together all of our thinking on how you can be marketed for maximum results. The plan will cover the areas as explained. This plan is presented... along with the resumes we have professionally written... in an executive briefing of several hours (in person... or via teleconferences).

RULE #13

Follow 5 Key Proven Rules
For Interviewing Success.

Be able to develop chemistry... find out what's important to the decision maker... tell memorable stories... deal with any objections and project the right image

1st—Develop positive chemistry right at the start

Are interviews just question and answer sessions? This may happen, but an interview that turns into a good offer involves far more. Last year there were more than 300 million interviews, and no two were the same. So how do you prepare? Compare this to a sports contest—there were millions of them and none were the same. In an interview or a contest, you can't plan exactly how things will go, but you can have a game plan for coming out on top.

We guide clients in achieving personal chemistry with executives of all personalities. Here are some ways to make sure that you build maximum chemistry with everyone.

1. Researching the firm helps build chemistry

Did you ever meet a person for the first time who knew a lot about you? It takes you by surprise, doesn't it? It's a great way to make a positive first impression. One friend of mine, an attorney, attributes his success to research he does ahead of time. Four out of every five of his clients tell him that he wins their business because he knows a lot more about them than anyone else does. When you arrange an appointment, use the opportunity to gather more information. Many people have been able to get job descriptions and brochures ahead of time simply by requesting them over the phone. Make it your business to not only know the firm's website, but go further to learn about their industry and the person you will be meeting.

2. Impressing the front office builds chemistry

Building chemistry with the front office staff can also make a difference. Can you guess what percentage of executives say their secretaries influence them? One-third? One-half? Well, about two-thirds of them do.

Not too long ago, I was interrupted by Carol, who stated that Mr. Baxter had arrived for his interview. I had forgotten about the appointment, and it was a busy day. I immediately asked, *"What do you think of him, Carol?"* She didn't say a word. She just gave a thumbs-down signal. That was the end for poor Baxter. No one ever taught him how important it is to make a positive impression on the front office staff. I told Carol to have him see one of our assistants, and to provide her opinion first. So, please be attentive to the front office staff.

3. Projecting the right image builds chemistry

When we are on the hiring end, many of us reach a negative decision in just a few minutes. Why? Well, if you have the credentials, you establish a good initial impression or you don't. And what determines chemistry? People silently react to the image you project, your dress, your posture and body language, the things you say about any subject, and the way you answer questions. Each of us is continually projecting some kind of image. It isn't just physical or dress either, although your appearance speaks before you say a word. It's also a matter of attitude and enthusiasm, and whether you project integrity.

4. Paying compliments builds chemistry

Do you like compliments? Do you think others do? You bet they do! So, before the interview, read or talk to people about the firm and uncover some good things to say. Then, let the interviewer know that you heard good things.

You can compliment their facilities, people, ads or many other things. However, be specific. Don't just say that people you know are impressed by their product. Talk about why they are impressed. All of us like to hear about how our products have pleased customers. By giving details, you show that you have given the subject some thought, and that your compliment is not just empty flattery.

5. Build chemistry when you ask questions

Ideally, we like our clients to be asking questions for a good portion of every interview. This enables them to assert some control and reduces interviewing pressure.

Now, the way you ask questions and the specific nature of their content will tell a lot about you. For this reason, we want each of our clients to have a questioning strategy. Most importantly, by asking intelligent questions, you will build your image in the eyes of the interviewer—and you will be building chemistry. You want him thinking, "Certainly, John seems very sharp, well informed… impressive." Of course, among the key questions you ask should be ones which are designed to find out what is "wrong" with the job or the company.

You might consider these "offensive questions" as opposed to "defensive questions" when you are fielding the answers. Often, we develop a host of key questions which our clients use over and over through all of their interviews. The point to keep in mind is that they need to be questions which, from the perspective of the interviewer, will get right to the heart of what is going on in the organization.

The types of questions you might ask

- Does the CEO have strong convictions about the approach needed to meet your goals in this area?

- How closely does R & D and sales work on new projects?

- If I were to become VP, how much input would you expect on selecting new products?

- Do you have a strong team in place, or will you expect me to recruit my own team?

- You need to have new capabilities to achieve your goals. Would I be given a free hand to do that, or would that cause political problems?

- Is top management unanimous on the need to develop new lines quickly, or are there strong differences of opinion?

- Would you see the major thrust as positioning the firm for a public offering... or a merger?

- Given the fact that you are #3 in your market right now, what is the timetable for improving your future?

6. Build chemistry when you answer questions

Keep in mind that the interviewer wants someone who can do the job, and wants to find that person in a minimum of time. The *way* you answer questions has more to do with building chemistry than *what* you say. For example, suppose you get the old standby, the number one question in the world of interviewing: *"Tell me about yourself."*

You'll want to answer, but chances are you're not sure what they want to hear. You could start out by talking about the kind of person you are and some of your attributes, but that may not be what the interviewer is interested in.

Faced with such a dilemma, a safe way out is to self-qualify your answer: *"Charles, I'd be happy to tell you about myself, and I'm sure you are interested in my work experience. I'll focus on the past few years and how they relate to your position. I can start with my most recent experience if you like."*

When you self-qualify, you give the interviewer an opportunity to respond, and to direct the conversation to another area. That way, you can avoid talking for ten minutes about the wrong things. Be prepared and have your own 60- to 120-second commercial ready.

When you answer questions, gear your comments to potential contributions related to sales, profits, cost reduction, innovations, etc. When there is a silence, make sure you have prepared some questions in advance. Create an opportunity to demonstrate knowledge. Being prepared builds confidence and allows you to be more spontaneous. Always maintain eye contact, and establish your sincerity and integrity.

When you encounter difficult questions, use the "U-turn" technique. For example, *"You look very impressive on paper, Marge. If you're this good, you ought to be able to solve all of our problems. Tell me, why should we hire you?"*

Now, of course, you know the person doesn't believe you're that good! However, if you begin to talk about why they should hire you, you run the real risk of going on about all the wrong things. With the "U-turn" technique, you don't give an answer. Instead, turn the question around in a way that acknowledges the status of the interviewer and pays an indirect compliment.

A comment might go like this: *"I have a lot of experience I think you could use. But it would be presumptuous of me to tell you what you need before I've shown the courtesy of listening to what you think the priorities are. If you'd be kind enough to share some of your thoughts on them, perhaps I could give a more intelligent answer."*

McKenzie Scott clients on chemistry

- *"Most of my interviews were with medium-sized firms in Arizona. Their selection processes were heavy on personal fit, chemistry with others and attitude."*

- *"Chemistry is where it's at. When it's down to a few candidates, competency will rarely prove to be the issue."*

- *"Obviously, being able to get connected to openings is important, but in the final stages working at building chemistry with everyone you meet is just as important."*

2nd—Find out what's most important to the decision maker

Sometimes interviewers will get directly to the point and tell you exactly what they are looking for. In most cases, you will need to ask some questions. Find out what happened to the last person in the job. Ask about his experiences and those of his superiors. Find out to whom the position reports and how long that person was in the job. And ask… *"What would be the biggest challenge I would face?"* Find out how the interviewer sees the problem, what the expectations are, and what progress has been made. Of course, once you find out what's most important to the firm… you need to tell them that you have what they want.

3rd—Tell memorable stories
that set you apart

In these stories, you need to indicate positive things you did to help organizations. For example, how you helped management meet goals, and the results you achieved. Show how you demonstrated a skill or a personal quality.

Develop SOAR stories that cover situations where you can demonstrate the value of fresh thinking as a means to improve productivity, or show that you have solved a variety of problems in diverse areas. Employers need to feel that you are the answer to one of their problems. If you can show them how you met or exceeded the needs in other places, they may conclude that you can do the same for them.

The idea is to create stories that demonstrate the benefits you bring. Remember, your "tickets" alone (degrees, titles, etc.) will not necessarily motivate another employer to hire you. You must use *action words* and *phrases* that add interest beyond your credentials. In the final analysis, employers hire people for what those phrases imply.

4th—Surface and deal
with any objections

Your next key to interviewing is to be able to overcome objections in a smooth and seamless way. With today's competition, if you stumble, there are too many others the employer can turn to. So, why play this by ear? Here is a simple method for handling objections, the "ARTS method." The letters stand for the following:

A Acknowledge the objection.
R Redirect the person's concern.
T Test to be sure you've removed the concern.
S Use a story to make your point.

Whenever someone raises an objection, the tension level rises. In step one you want to reduce the tension level.

A   Acknowledge the objection

"I can understand your concern, and I would like to address it for you." Or *"You've raised an interesting point. It deserves some frank discussion."* The phrases are not so important— it's the feeling you impart. You have acted in a reassuring way; it's clear that you feel secure about your abilities.

R   Redirect their concern

Let's say the interviewer raised the fact that your experience was in a different industry. *"What qualities are you looking for in an ideal candidate that prompted this concern?"*

Now, you can't do too much about that, but you can show that you are someone who contributes quickly (e.g., *"When you raise that question, I understand that you want to be sure the person you put in this job is someone who will contribute quickly. Isn't that it?"*) The interviewer will reaffirm that you are indeed correct. With just a little thought, it is easy to refocus the conversation toward the positive qualities that are really on the interviewer's mind.

T   Use a testing question to see
if you have removed their concern

Here is an example of asking a testing question: *"If I could show that I could contribute quickly, even when learning new information, would that help?"* After you get a positive response, you can go directly to your answer, or you can introduce one of your key strengths. You might say: *"If I could show you that I work well under pressure, might that ease your concern somewhat?"*

S   Use a supporting story to confirm your point

The final thing to do is to use a supporting story as part of your answer, ending it with a question that will keep the conversation positive. Remember, what really counts is the fact that you did not get flustered. If you've done it right, interviewers won't be that concerned about your exact answer. They'll be thinking, *"This person handled that situation very well."*

Note: Bear in mind that an objection is really a sign of interest. If the employer were not interested, he or she would not even bother asking you to overcome the objection.

Other basics
for interviewing

- Avoid arriving too early for appointments. At lunch take your cue on drinks and avoid smoking.

- Never read mail on someone's desk or look at your watch. Avoid discussions on religion or politics. Never be a braggart and rarely name-drop. Also, don't criticize past employers, and never be negative about anything.

- Don't let an interview carry on too long. When a discussion peaks, diplomatically lead to an end of the meeting. Never linger afterward.

- Emphasize recent experiences, use recent stories and project diversified interests and a strong work ethic. There will always be questions for which you won't have answers. Don't let it bother you.

- Don't be controlling. Keep your eye on body language. Read between the lines. Find a way to answer questions that should have been asked, but were not!

- Follow up every interview with an enthusiastic letter that emphasizes why you are a "good fit."

30 questions you
may need to answer

If you want to be at your best, be sure to have answers prepared to these common questions. Any that you are uncertain about should be checked and brought up with our staff.

- *Why are you leaving? Why have you stayed so long?*
- *What's wrong with your present firm?*
- *What are your capabilities that will help us?*
- *What major challenges have you faced?*
- *What references can you give us?*
- *Which jobs have you enjoyed the most? Why?*
- *How well do you handle pressure?*
- *What do you think of your ex-boss?*
- *Why haven't you found a job so far?*
- *Can you fit into an unstructured environment?*
- *Why do you want to work for us?*
- *What are your greatest accomplishments?*
- *Describe your management style.*
- *What is your biggest strength? Weakness?*
- *How do you handle confrontation?*
- *How often have you had raises? Your compensation?*
- *Why aren't you earning more at your age?*
- *How would a close friend describe you?*
- *Have you ever been arrested or convicted?*
- *How good is your health?*
- *How do you spend your spare time? Your hobbies?*
- *What was the last book you read?*
- *Have you ever been refused a bond? Been bankrupt?*
- *Tell me about yourself.*
- *How strong is your financial situation?*
- *What people do you admire?*
- *Where else are you interviewing? Other offers received?*
- *If you could start over, what would you do differently?*
- *How would others describe your work ethic?*

5th—Present the right image
... dress guidelines for women

Clothes tell the employer how you see yourself. Your hairstyle and your choice of makeup is either going to reinforce or detract from your professional image. The accessories you choose—shoes, purse, jewelry—make a further statement about your awareness of that image. There is no single look for all women. Guidelines about dress have become more flexible. "Presence" involves not only appearance, but also self confidence and knowledge. Here are some guidelines.

Hairstyle and makeup... nails and perfume

A good haircut is essential. Short to medium length hair is most appropriate. Keep away from an "extreme" look—anything frizzy, too full, teased or too long. Your makeup should appear natural. If you have never worn makeup, recognize that most people feel their appearance can be enhanced by some foundation, a touch of blush, a light lipstick, and some mascara.

Your nails should be medium length and filed attractively. No squares or points. Keep to an oval shape. Keep away from overly distracting shades, even though they may be fashionable at the time. If you are accustomed to wearing fragrance, don't use anything overpowering.

Clothing for interviews

A well tailored suit is always appropriate for an interview. When choosing colors, keep to an understated, conservative look. A solid color, a muted tweed or plaid, or a subtle pinstripe is always in good taste. You want your next employer to remember you, not your outfit. If you generally wear bright or bold colors, choose a scarf or blouse in a shade you enjoy. Blouses or sweaters to go with your suit should either be white, off white, beige, or a color complementary to your suit. A solid color dress, properly tailored and well fitting, is also appropriate for interviewing. A subtle plaid or stripe can also be correct. Since skirt lengths vary, select a length in keeping with the overall style of suit or dress you are wearing. Times change, and there are always exceptions, but a good rule of thumb is nothing shorter than an inch below your knee.

Shoes, stockings, briefcases and jewelry

Generally, stockings should be in a neutral shade, seamless, and snug fitting. Stockings in a complementary shade to your outfit are periodically in fashion and would also be acceptable. Stay away from heavily textured or patterned stockings. The leather of the shoes you select should be well polished. Keep away from clogs, sandals, and platform soled shoes.

If you plan to carry a briefcase, put your handbag items in it. You don't want to appear too "laden down." Keep your jewelry simple and of good quality. The key is never to use anything so startling that it detracts from the impression you want to make. Never wear a handful of rings.

Your general appearance

There is an unspoken "managerial" dress code for women. It is more tailored than feminine (no plunging necklines or sheer fabrics) and enhances a ""power" look. These emphasize a woman's ability to perform on the job, rather than femininity. Make sure you look like you are ready for the income level to which you aspire. Body language is also important. Straight posture says that you take pride in your appearance.

Present the right image
... dress guidelines for men

Looking good means feeling good and feeling confident. Before you launch your search, assess your wardrobe. You need several outfits because you must expect to go through a series of two, three, or more interviews. Use your clothing to project a personality that fits the situation and the firm.

Suits and shirts

Most people will do best if their suits are properly fitted and conservative. One of the most difficult things for most men to do is throw away suits. The time for such action may be now. Before you make a purchase, prepare for your fitting by deciding how you will wear the suit. Allow for nothing in the pockets except a few bills and some change. When interviewing, your wallet can be kept in a briefcase.

Another important observation relates to the length of your jacket sleeve. Allow 5" from the top of your thumb to the end of your sleeve. Don't let tailors persuade you to take longer sleeves!

Clothing must fit properly. Go back at least twice for alterations. Allow for some slight shrinkage in dry cleaning. The front of your pants cuff should barely touch the shoe.

Regarding the fit of your shirt, if you have gained a significant amount of weight, you may be wearing your collar too tight. Ex-athletes who have trimmed down will often find that their collars have become loose.

Generally speaking, you will want to avoid short sleeved shirts. Those who wear cuff links should make sure they are simple. A gaudy look is likely to be perceived as a negative.

Ties, shoes & accessories

Ties can be fun and can give you a unique look. To a great extent, this element of your wardrobe is a matter of preference. Above all, be sure your tie is clean. Bow ties do little to enhance most people's image.

Your shoes should be well polished and light to medium in weight. Slip-ons are increasingly acceptable. The old military "spitshine" is still a real power builder.

Don't underrate accessories. Belts and belt buckles should be conservative. Socks should be over the calf in length and normally a solid color complementing the suit. It is not necessary to have a handkerchief nicked in your breast pocket, but it can be a nice touch. A wallet and briefcase show a lot about a man. Thin wallets and neat briefcases are a nice complement to your overall appearance.

Your general appearance

As a rule, if you appear older than you would like, your hair should be on the short side. For most men in their 20s or 30s, however, a somewhat longer look is appropriate.

A clean shave is a must. For late afternoon interviews, carry an electric razor in your briefcase. As far as after-shave or cologne is concerned, keep it subtle. For those of you who are overweight, clothes can cover up just so much. Try to lose some extra pounds if possible. If not, stand up straight and sit tall. Obviously, you want to look your best at all times.

Sample answers to
common questions

What is your biggest weakness?

"Well, I really don't feel I have any major weaknesses which affect my working ability. At times I have a tendency to be impatient about getting things done."

Why are you leaving?

"I want to earn more, have added responsibility, and expand my knowledge in my field. These opportunities don't exist in my present firm."

You haven't worked in our industry before. When could you make a contribution?

"I expect to be able to make a contribution in a short time. Obviously, it will take some time to get my feet wet. However, there are a number of things I have accomplished before, and I may be able to institute some of them once I gain a better understanding of your firm. I'm a quick learner."

How long would you stay with us?

"As I mentioned to you, I'm looking for a career. However, I'm a realist. If I don't do the job, you won't want me around; and if there is no opportunity, it won't be right for me."

What's wrong with your current firm?

"I don't feel there is anything wrong with the firm. I have enjoyed working there, and they have some really top people. It's a good company, but I am ready for some added responsibility and challenge."

What are your short range objectives?

Keep your answer focused on the job for which you are interviewing. It is not in your best interest to pick short range objectives that the job or company might be unable to provide.

What are your long range objectives?
In dealing with this question, it is a good idea to remain flexible. A brief answer that refers to moving up the ladder as quickly and as far as your capabilities permit, will suffice.

How good is your health?
The obvious answer is that your health is fine. You should go on to state that you are accustomed to working long hours and are quite capable of keeping up a fast pace. If you have a health problem that the interviewer could easily find out about, then give a truthful answer. However, you should go on to point out that your condition has had no adverse effect on performance, attendance or ability to give 100%.

How long would it take you to make a contribution?
This question may be the interviewer's way of saying he is concerned about your lack of experience in his industry. Indicate that you are confident of your ability to contribute rapidly and support your claim with a SOAR story.

**If you could start your career
over, what would you do differently?**
"On the whole I would have to say that I am extremely proud of my achievements and quite happy with my career progression to date."

What do you think of your boss?
Obviously, if you think your boss is great, then it is pretty easy to answer this question. On the other hand, if you really didn't get along with your boss, then responding to this question becomes challenging. The interview is not the place to discuss the shortcomings of your boss. Doing so will make you sound like a whiner or troublemaker. Instead, comment briefly on some positive aspects of your boss, be they in his personality or her management style... and leave it at that.

Why haven't you found a job so far?
Being apologetic or simply saying that it's a tough market in your field will not help you. Depending upon the length of your unemployment, it may be enough to respond that you are not seeking a job, but are selectively looking for the right career opportunity and have not yet found it.

What was the last book you read, movie you saw, or sporting event you attended?
Some think these types of questions provide information about your personality and interests. Unless the movie or book is controversial, tell the truth. But, it's important that you have read, seen, or attended whatever you claimed, since more detailed questioning may follow.

What are your biggest accomplishments in your present or last job?
In citing your accomplishments, pick those that seem to line up well with the major elements of the position under consideration. For example, if you have accomplishments in both cost and general accounting, and you're interviewing for a general accounting position, you obviously want to bias your answer toward the position for which you are a candidate. The goal is to always show the interviewer that your accomplishments line up with the company needs.

What interests you most about our position?... the least?
The response to the former should be an aspect or aspects of the job that benefit the employer, not you. For example, you might cite the challenge of the problems to be solved, or the opportunity to apply your skills to particular challenges. For the second question, you might say, "At this point I have not heard anything about the job that turns me off."

Why aren't you earning more at your age?
If you are in a low paying industry, make sure that you point out that you have received performance raises. Also point out that your industry/function is traditionally low paying, which is one of the reasons you are looking for a new job. When discussing how much you are making, respond in terms of value of the job. For example, you might say… "My position has a range that goes from _____ to _____ and I am well over the midpoint. Because of performance, I'm one of the better paid in the firm."

What do your subordinates think of you?
This is an opportunity for you to sell yourself through another person's viewpoint. Offer strengths and attributes that are relevant to your ability to perform well in the position for which you're being considered.

Why do you want to work for us?
If this question is asked very early in the interview, you may not really have a good answer. Therefore, give a response instead like this: Based on what I learned about your organization from people I know, I did some research and found that you've achieved impressive sales increases for the last six quarters. Given that kind of growth, I felt that my strong background in _____ might be valuable to you.

Successful interviewing depends on how well you can build chemistry and find out what's important to the employer... and how well you can tell stories, overcome objections and project the right image.

How McKenzie Scott helps with rule #13
Follow 5 key proven rules
for interviewing success

Our team works with you throughout all interviews. This includes sharing suggestions to any concerns that may arise. With our research service, you can get information about employers before interviews. Other market intelligence includes:

- Company and market trend reports
- Investment banker reports on firms / industries
- Background profiles on 800,000 executives
- Trade magazine analysts' reports
- In-depth financial information on firms

RULE #14

Use a 7-Step Negotiation Formula
to Increase Your Financial Package.

**Know when to negotiate, what to negotiate and how
to negotiate. The key is to follow this proven formula
based on common sense and soft selling.**

Since most people seldom face a personal negotiating
experience, it should come as no surprise that few of us are
real experts at negotiating for ourselves. While they may be
excellent company negotiators, we have seen many strong
people leave serious money on the table when it came to
negotiating their own package.

Now, the first thing you need to decide... is when to start a
negotiation process. Some people mistakenly think negotiation
is a continuous selling situation that occurs throughout their
interviews. However, before you ever attempt to negotiate,
you have to make sure that the employer is "sold on you."
Furthermore, you want an offer to be extended.

Once an offer has been presented, you can't begin to negotiate unless there is some hope that you can get the employer
to offer new terms. This is something that you need to sense
on an individual basis. From that point on, your sincerity and
credibility will be essential.

What to Negotiate

Coming to grips with what should be negotiated is, of course, different for everyone. Not too long ago we handled a marketing executive from Kellogg in Michigan. His primary goal was to have his family move to a new area that met outdoor lifestyle requirements, and he started by suggesting to us that a 20% reduction in income would be acceptable.

However, after a three-month search, he accepted a top position with a firm in Boca Raton. When we finished helping with his negotiations, his compensation ended up 15% higher, and he received a signing bonus, as well.

Another executive was with J & J. He wanted out of the major corporation environment. He left his large company career behind when he landed with a venture capital group. His assignment was to oversee ventures that the firm funded by serving as acting CEO. He was to complete the initial setup, find a permanent CEO, and then move on to another assignment, but remain on the board.

Based in Castle Pines, Colorado, he will handle two ventures simultaneously for six-month periods—eight over two years. His base of $200,000 was a considerable decrease, but if just one firm goes public, his equity benefit will be in the many millions. Needless to say, the final staging of his executive level negotiations didn't just happen. In the chapter that follows, the basics of our negotiation system are outlined in the most simple terms.

Some basics to consider

Base salary and signing bonus. When you make a change, you want to expect a total package that is 20%+... more than where you were. Other elements include such things as commissions, medical and life insurance, annual bonus based on meeting performance goals, profit sharing and pension plans. If you negotiate profit sharing, know the accounting.

Exit strategy. Standard agreements cover a minimum of six months' to a year's severance, and are triggered if the firm lessens your responsibilities.

Stock option purchase plans. If you purchase stock at market price, the company may buy an equal amount under your name up to a percentage of your income.

Stock grants. You will most likely be obligated for taxes based upon the market value.

ISOs (incentive stock options). This is an option to purchase a certain number of shares at market value on a given day, generally exercisable years away. The primary value of ISOs is that should you eventually buy them, no tax is due on the day of purchase… as you pay only on your capital gains when your shares are sold.

Restricted stock units. Stock units are pegged in value, e.g., as one share of stock for every five units. The key is when you can convert to cash or shares.

Phantom stock options and stock appreciation rights. Rights to receive the difference in market value between the time granted and value when converted.

Non-qualified stock options. This is an option to purchase stock below market prices. Tax will be due on the difference between the price at which you exercise your right of purchase and the market value of the stock.

Relocation expenses. This can include house purchase, moving expenses, mortgage rate differential, real estate, closing costs, cost of bridge loan, trips to look for a home, lodging fees, tuition, and spouse reemployment services.

Other perks. These can include automobile lease, luncheons, athletic/country club membership, child care, physical exam, disability pay, legal assistance, product discounts, dining room privileges, financial planning assistance, tuition reimbursement, CPA and tax assistance, short-term loans, insurance benefits after termination, special reimbursement for foreign service, outplacement assistance and deferred compensation.

If you don't have any success in your negotiations, then shift from the "present" and focus instead on futures: a review after six months, a better title, an automatic increase after time. These are easier things to get.

Contracts. The following are usually incorporated: the length of the agreement, your specific assignment, your title, location, to whom you report, your compensation and what happens if there is a merger or if you are fired. It should also cover the specific items on the negotiation list that are part of your package.

Any agreement you accept should cover all nonlegal situations under which an employer may choose to terminate you. Signing bonuses and generous severance packages are moving into all income levels—especially when there is a relocation.

How to negotiate... our 7 simple steps

This advice is based on the fact that our staff is constantly involved with dozens of negotiations. We work on deals in every part of the country. This system is based on that experience and is a soft sell method which involves negotiating with skill and dignity. The advice has meant tens of thousands of dollars to many people.

Negotiating step #1... be sincere and reasonable... never cold or calculating

In the job-search situation, intimidation and attack strategies have no value. Here, you're setting the tone for a long-term relationship. In fact, most people don't like negotiation because they associate it with confrontation and role playing, something that does not come naturally. The best negotiators are prepared and never cause irritation. Make sure to be sincere and reasonable, never cold or calculating.

As you approach your negotiations, it is essential you have clear ideas about what you want. Realizing you will not achieve everything, you will want to keep your main objectives in mind, and never risk an entire negotiation by coming on too strong about less important points. Of course, when you are ready to negotiate, the easiest way to "frame and strengthen" your position is to clarify that you have been exploring some other opportunities that also have a certain appeal.

Negotiating step #2... avoid premature income discussions

You need to avoid the hard lessons we see others experiencing every day. Here's an example. One client was a general manager with Exxon, earning a sizeable income, but wanting to win a new job at a 20% increase. After two meetings, the CEO said, *"Bill, we'd like to have you join us, and I'd like to work out something attractive for you. What have you been used to earning at Exxon?"*

At that point, having been encouraged, Bill explained his income. To make a long story short, he accepted a position. However, he later found out that the last person had been paid 40% more, and the company fully expected to match it. Now, the moral is that you should never negotiate based on where you've been. Negotiation is like poker. You never want to lay your earnings on the table!

Premature discussions about money can be a real deal breaker. Besides, the more enthusiastic an employer becomes about you, the more likely he'll be willing to pay more. Sometimes an interviewer will begin like this: *"Jim, before we get started, I'd like to know how much money you are looking for."* Here is a possible response: *"Charles, I could talk more intelligently about my circumstances after I know more about the job. Will this job have line responsibilities?"*

Or, *"Charles, I would not take your time if I did not have a fairly good idea of the range you could pay. If we can agree that my experience fits your needs, I doubt we'll have a problem on compensation. My concern is whether your needs call for someone with my background."* Here, the idea is to remain gracious while avoiding a direct answer. If an interviewer persists, say: *"I'd rather avoid discussing compensation. Challenge is most important to me, and I would like to talk money after we both feel I'm right for the job."* If all else fails, give a range surrounding your estimate of what the job pays.

Negotiating step #3...
never commit when you get an offer

When offered a job, take the opportunity to praise the firm and explain that you need some time to consider it. *"Charles, I am pleased you made me an offer. This is an outstanding firm, and the position has great promise. I am sure you can appreciate that I would like some time to give it further consideration. It would not present any problem, would it, if I were to get back to you on Monday?"* Our standard recommendation for almost all clients is to get the offer in writing and ask for seven days to respond. In some cases we advise people to respond quicker.

When you call back, open with some positive statements, then raise the possibility of redefining the job. *"Charles, with kids entering college, I had done some planning based on an income that was $10,000 higher. Would it be possible to take another look at the job specs? For my part, I know that if you could make a modest additional investment, my performance will show you a handsome return. I sincerely hope that we can make some adjustment. Can we take a look at it?"*

Of course, if you are happy with the job, but would like to raise the salary, use the same technique, but show vulnerability, then suggest that a dollar figure be added to the base.

Normally, if that figure is within 15% of what you have been offered, the employer will not take offense and will grant you part of it. Of course, asking for more money is a negative, and needs to be balanced by positives. Consider the following: *"Charles, I cannot tell you how pleased I am. The challenge is there, and I think my experience is perfect. There is one problem, however. You see, one of the main reasons I wanted to make a change was for financial balance. Can you see your way clear to adding $10,000 to the base? It would ease my family situation considerably."*

Negotiating step #4...
learn how to use vulnerability

Expressing a slight amount of vulnerability can be a powerful weapon. Just let the employer know that accepting the job as offered would cause you some personal difficulties. When you use this strategy, it plays to their desire to make you happy. Be flattered by the offer, but say that you may have to disappoint your family in order to afford the job:

"I love the job and really want to join you, but we'd have some difficulty because of the options I will be losing. Is there a chance you could go a little higher?"

Questioning, rather than demanding, is the rule. The best negotiators persuade through questions. This gives them needed information to gain control. It also gives them time to think and not put their cards on the table. Good negotiators will not say, *"I do not agree with you because…"* Rather, they will say, *"Charles, you do make a good point, but I wonder if there is room for another view."* They would never say, *"That would not be any good for me."* They might say, *"Charles, could you tell me how you think this would work for me?"*

Then they will follow up with questions, so the employer can discover that their proposal is not quite enough. If your questions lead them to discover they were wrong, they will be disposed to changing the terms.

Negotiating step #5...
negotiate the job responsibilities

Reshape the job into a larger one, and the range will be higher. To get started, begin with a positive comment about the job and the firm and suggest they might benefit by adding responsibilities to the job. Then offer to share your thoughts. For example, *"Charles, there is no doubt this is a good job. However, based on what you have told me, I could be even more helpful if a few related elements were added. There are three areas where my experience could make a difference. I'd like to discuss them so we can see if they could be included in the job description."*

You could then go on to talk about the areas where the firm might capitalize on your experience, showing with stories how you made contributions before. If the interviewer agrees these are important, have them added to the job description. Believe it or not, reshaping the job can often be just that simple! Can you see how we have applied basic principles here? There was no confrontation.

Negotiating step #6... introduce
other things on which to base the offer

This can include the importance of the job to the firm, what you would make with a raise where you are, your total compensation package, what you believe the market is for your background, or other offers you are considering.

In the example that follows, notice how there are no demands, only questions. By inviting employers to explore the situation, you are giving them the freedom to reach their own conclusions about whether their offer is too low. Using this approach, you come across as enthusiastic, sincere, and slightly vulnerable—never as cold or calculating, or as someone who is putting them in a corner. Your comment might be:

"Charles, let me first tell you once again how pleased I am over the offer. I feel very positive about the prospect of joining you, and I can only say that my enthusiasm has continued to increase. This is the job I want. It's a situation where I could look forward to staying with the firm for the long term.

"There is one hurdle that I have to overcome. You see, I've been underpaid for some time, and it has created a situation where I need to start earning at a rate reflecting my ability to contribute. If I stayed where I am, I'd be due for a raise, which would put me close to your offer.

"In talking with other firms, I've discovered that some realize this, and they have mentioned ranges that are 25% higher. Now, I don't want to work for them—I want to work for you. But I do have some pressing needs. Perhaps the firm could approve a higher offer. Can we pursue this together?"

Negotiating step #7...
use your enthusiasm throughout

If you load maximum enthusiasm into your statements, it becomes nearly impossible for the employer to conclude that you should not be with them. Enthusiasm assumes even more importance when you have been underpaid. Ideally, an offer should be based on your value to the company, but in reality, most employers will base their offers on present earnings.

How a few clients used this
7-step system for negotiation

■ *"I joined a nationally known nonprofit in a #2 capacity. The initial offer was $210K. Over three weeks we raised this to $245K. All moving expenses and an excellent exit package were incorporated."*

■ *"My new position is manager of a large sporting goods store. We negotiated a financial package that is worth 30% more to me in the first year alone."*

■ *"An M.D., I left a medical center to join a pharmaceutical firm known for its R & D capability. Guaranteed salary and bonus were equal to my previous earnings, but the stock grant and future options may cover my retirement."*

■ *"As an attorney I decided to leave my law firm. I negotiated an operations job in a small service firm along with General Counsel responsibilities. My package was 27% more."*

Typical executive level
negotiation situations

Situation #1

The chairman of a firm in the investment world sent our client a short e-mail with an offer of a $300,000 base, plus bonus potential, plus a reasonably attractive package of options. Once the chairman made the offer, he turned it over to his general counsel. Our client retained a top law firm to represent him, and our first assignment was to strategize and draft his initial counter proposal. The next ten days involved a series of discussions by all parties. We could see that the general counsel was under great pressure to get the deal done. Our senior staff took the lead in phone conferences, which included our client, his attorney and the general counsel. We, rather than the client, communicated the client's needs, and the rationale behind our request. To educate the firm, we presented a written analysis of several other deals, and an option package our client had available.

Situation #2

A client earning $250,000 was offered a position by a firm being pursued in an acquisition. In this case, the senior HR executive took the negotiating lead. We were successful in getting an initial offer of $350,000 raised to $400,000. In addition, we negotiated a $50,000 signing bonus in lieu of relocation assistance. The key was to move the corporation up by educating them to the current market, and other deals that were going down. Because risks of acquisition were involved, we focused on an attractive severance package... one that amounted to two years of income and immediate vesting of stock options.

When an offer is received, consider these negotiation goals

- Get your job responsibilities expanded into a larger job
- Increase your initial salary offer by 10-30%
- Secure a package of benefits that's right for you
- Negotiate a signing bonus up to 10-25% of your salary
- Negotiate some form of stock options

Negotiating your
best financial package
will be much easier—if you
simply rely on this 7-step
formula we have outlined.

**How McKenzie Scott helps with rule #14
Use a 7-step negotiation formula
to increase your financial package**

This simple but proven formula has helped people at every income level negotiate a far better package than they would have otherwise achieved. We use our experience with thousands of other negotiations to assist in our implementation of these principles. Typically, we help strategize every offer that is received and suggest appropriate verbal and written responses. For certain high level clients, on an optional basis, we take an active role... participating on their behalf—and representing them in the negotiation process itself.

RULE #15

Build An Unstoppable
Will To Succeed.

Approach success as being inevitable. Your positive attitude will help you do it sooner rather than later.

A positive attitude is the most common thread among all winners. It will separate you from the many who give up, settle for less, or stay in unattractive situations. It's easy to build a will to succeed if you follow six basic guidelines.

1. Develop positive beliefs about yourself

Now is a good time to remind yourself of all the good things you have done. It starts with your past, naturally. Write down positive things "you've done and can do." Make it as long and complete as possible. You will find it reassuring. It will begin to provide reinforcement for the positive attitude you must maintain. All you need are short sentences.

For example: I have increased profits. I have attracted new business. I have cut costs, etc. Here are some "can do's" to consider: I can work with all levels of people. I can get things done quickly. I can motivate others, and so forth. They also reflect your *skill sets* as described earlier in this text. Once you've prepared these lists, you will begin to realize just what value you will have for your next employer.

2. Get rid of negative beliefs

Having built a set of positive beliefs about yourself, your second step is to get rid of beliefs that might inhibit your will to succeed. Are you saying, "things are bad, it's a grim world out there." If so, this simply reflects your beliefs about "the way you think things really are." If you believe the economy is bad, you will see breaking news and pay attention to layoffs or sales declines. On the other hand, if you believe that there are many areas of opportunity, then you will notice new firms, new products and the like.

3. Set your future expectations higher

Our expectations have a lot to do with the way things happen for us. Obvious examples are the many sports teams and athletes who, when asked about their success, often reply, *"We expected all along that we would win."*

But it isn't only sports teams. A close look at the lives of leaders in almost any field reveals a common theme. Whether it's a leading scientist, educator, salesperson, movie personality, or leader of industry, you'll find that each of them had very positive expectations of themselves.

All motivational speakers and inspirational leaders tell us that it is possible to work on our expectations by visualizing good things happening to us. Picture yourself setting and achieving high goals. Positive visualizations can become a continuous process of reinforcement that will give you a new-found power and self confidence.

4. Put your positive expectations to work now

Your fourth step in building a will to succeed is putting your positive expectations to work right away. For instance, if someone tells you that an interview can take only 15 minutes, recognize it's a screening interview and build expectations that it will allow you to showcase your potential.

Let's take another example. Suppose you had an excellent interview, called twice afterwards, and got no response. Don't assume they have lost interest. Instead, assume they're busy, that most people don't really get back when they say they will, and that they are still very interested.

Decide now, that your second meeting will be better than the first. With that kind of expectation, you will then find it easy to write a short follow-up note that your interest continues to grow, and that you are dedicated to becoming the best ever in the job. In this instance, your expectations affect your actions, and they affect the results. In that way, your will to succeed can and does make things happen.

5. Project a positive attitude to everyone

Start by talking to people about your positive expectations. When you do this, it reaffirms your own commitment. You have put yourself on the line.

Let these ideas flow into your general attitude, and begin to reach out and help others. Why? Once again, experts tell us this is a give and get world. Eventually, it reaches the point where it becomes obvious to anyone who meets you, that you project a lot of confidence about yourself.

You'll have to work at this, but it's easy and it's fun. A spring in your step, a firm handshake, a confident look in your eye, and comments which reveal a positive outlook can all help you project good feelings to the outside world.

6. Make things happen by getting into action

If you look at achievers in any field, you will find that they are very active people. It's a simple fact that taking action is in itself like taking an energy tonic.

Choose any kind of example you like. The head of a college breathing new life into an institution, a company president turning around a money losing operation, a football coach turning a losing team into winners, a home run hitter in the act of swinging the bat, or a test pilot setting a new speed record. They are so intent on their actions, there is no room for doubt and indecision. You can do the same thing in your job search effort.

Optimism and positive mental attitude can have a major impact on you... as well as everyone you meet. It's contagious!

How McKenzie Scott helps with rule #15
Build an unstoppable
will to succeed

Our Marketing Directors, research or information services staff, or another member of our team—all initiate calls to you on a frequent basis. Helping you maintain a positive attitude is important. Besides expertise, our team will supply direction, careful listening, encouragement and emotional support.

Supplemental #1

Classic Career Situations: If One
Describes You... Gear Up Your Urgency.

Are you a young executive at a career crossroads?

These executives are typically 28-46 years old, BA/BS or MBA, doing well financially, either highly marketable and confident... or concerned because they have been blocked in middle or upper management for some time.

Many of these people are at one of the most important crossroads they will face. And, many potentially great careers are lost at this critical stage. Some, of course, are in a position of strength. They are confident and highly marketable. It's important for these executives to explore *all* their options when making a move... not just one or two.

On the other hand, some executives are less confident. They've found themselves blocked for some time. Some fail to discover the importance of broadening out before it's too late. Age is a factor here. They're well aware of the bottleneck at middle and lower upper management.

Some of these people are in situations where they have not attracted attention from top management. Other talented people may be just ahead of them—or they may not be aligned well enough politically. Because they value their careers so highly, a bad move at this stage can be tragic. They must make the right move.

The advantage of having an objective appraisal of their marketability and options can be critical. They need to uncover and be ready to market their full range of assets and transferable skills.

If some of these people don't control their careers now, they may lose the advantage of their good beginnings. They must stage their careers and plan their futures. Some are not far from falling into mediocrity, allowing a marketability decline. These people are often wise to consider new environments in smaller and medium-sized firms, and in emerging industries—where they can receive greater responsibility.

Working in an entrepreneurial environment and combining it with large corporate experience can be an excellent platform for future moves. It may also be time for some to take a calculated risk in trying to make a dramatic move up financially. They are ready to do their boss's job... and perhaps much better!

People like this often make the mistake of just dabbling in the market... answering ads, speaking with a few recruiters. The trouble is, that while they might surface something sooner or later, it's only one offer—requiring a one-shot leap of faith.

These people should develop and follow an action plan—one which gives them a structured system aimed at developing the right interviews. Good numbers are necessary because executives have to be realistic about rejections. And, the higher you go, the truer this is.

Are you a corporate officer in a bad career position?

The corporate officer—$100K to $750K+... age 36 to 62... often at the peak of their marketability. Job is threatened, challenge gone, or been terminated.

People in this position are often unsure about their futures. Normally in control, they sense changes ahead. A few may be concerned that they have wasted their best career opportunity. Others may be fed up with politics and want out entirely. Some worry their careers could be lost at this stage.

At higher levels, these people are often concerned about campaigning with dignity. They also feel that they cannot afford to make another mistake. Their next move often needs to be their last. Time may be their greatest enemy.

<u>One key rule of thumb:</u> Unemployment is a liability... and over time, you will dig yourself a deeper and deeper hole. Remember that the perception among employers is, good people don't last long in the market. For this reason, you need an aggressive campaign approach, or risk a bleak future.

There is a tendency for these professionals to have an exaggerated view of their marketability. A full marketability appraisal can be valuable, and chances are, they need to plan on getting much wider exposure than they realize.

Of course, for corporate officers at senior levels, the need for truly superior marketing materials is critical. They will make or break the success of their campaigns. For many, their entire backgrounds should also be reshaped in a narrative biography format. This makes it easier to attract interest from companies in new industries.

Will you be viewed as having had too many jobs?

Often, a client will come to us after several bad moves. Emotionally, they may be confused, and despite talent, they are doubting themselves. Frequently, they are in a poor state of mind.

Typically, this is where an executive is concerned and wondering if there is any hope. Is the problem with them, or are they a victim of circumstances? "Where in the world do I go from here?"

These people often have a lack of focus in terms of industry direction. They have begun to lose hope for the future. Some recognize that their careers are in shambles. Some feel lonely and vulnerable. If they examine their previous changes, they will see that bad moves in the past were made because they didn't professionally search. They took situations that just came their way.

These people need to control their career destiny. At this stage, mistakes must be avoided and a move made on a more scientific basis.

Historically, many have overreacted against past problems by taking the first thing that came along. However, the short-term *solution* turned out to be their long-term *problem*. For many, the key to success is in their ability to get connected to enough openings. Then, after the right strategic moves during interviews, they need to accept the right situation and stay with it.

Will you be viewed as having been too long in one firm or industry?

These people do not know what they are worth and may never have looked before. For this reason, the ability to expand their true marketability is paramount.

Given an honest choice, these people probably would not leave their current employer if they did not believe they were missing out on the things other people have—more income and challenge, recognition and future. Unless their lethargy is shaken, they may spend the best years of their lives with indecision. Action for these people may come too late to be meaningful. Often, in their own eyes, they are in danger of labeling themselves as *"less than the success they should have been."*

Sometimes, lack of confidence in their marketability may have been fostered by years of plodding in anonymity. The reality is that they are often quite marketable. Most of the time, these people are simply unaware of what's really out there for them. Not only are they unaware of what's out there, but employers will be ignorant of their value, because they have never prepared materials that truly qualify them for new directions. And whenever there's a problem of ignorance, the solution is communication.

The weight of these campaigns falls on their ability to build an appropriate bridge, from where they've been—to where they want to be… both through their resumes and communication in general. Their old resume often telegraphs their major liability—their one company or one industry experience—and has restricted their activity.

We get concerned that in this category, the longer they wait, the more difficult it is. In all likelihood, if they do not move soon, they should not change at all.

Are you a former entrepreneur facing a return to the market?

These executives recognize that certain employers will be hesitant to hire someone who has owned a business. They know there will be concerns about whether they may go back in their own business, whether they can be a team player in a corporate structure. They may also be viewed as failures, looking for a port in the storm.

Talented as they may be, former entrepreneurs face special challenges. Many are identified with a narrow industry, and they lack credibility outside that niche. Of course, some want, or need by virtue of non-compete agreements, to seek out positions in different industries. However, they are unsure of where they would fit.

Some, having achieved success, want to be in a business that has an explicit mission of enriching people's lives.

Often, this is a critical move for people. They have not done this before, and they need to do it right. They also are down-to-earth realists. To have credibility, they must have concrete "selling propositions," as well as "industry hooks" based on facts and the realities of the marketplace, not just vague generalities.

Entrepreneurs are seldom short on achievements. However, what they need are powerful written presentations that make them credible over a broader spectrum.

Are you someone for whom age might prove a major liability?

Many people have doubts about competing. Their age may be a barrier for the responsibility their pride and ego commands. Regrettably, if they believe age is the barrier, and remain unhappily employed elsewhere, this mental obstacle effectively blocks their putting forth the required energy to make the right move.

Many people use age as an excuse. Their confidence may be on the wane, and despite their experience, they don't really know how to search at their level.

Dealing with perceptions about age is like any other task. You progress if you take action. As you might suspect, action starts with their beliefs about themselves and what's possible. Barriers fall as their marketable skills are surfaced.

They come to understand that their marketability can be enhanced through communication of all the skills, know-how and personal strengths they possess.

If they can contribute, age is irrelevant. Employers think about themselves, their problems and their own challenges. Of course, age will eliminate people from opportunities. That's why aggressiveness is called for… and people need to put the numbers on their side.

When we work with these people, we look to identify all the credible industry hooks they possess—broadening the functions they can fill, and the industries they can target. Obviously, superior materials are essential. Then, our technology enables their credentials to be aggressively put into play.

While age will eliminate some options, it is also true that young executives look for veteran talent to add balance. Today, people in their late 40s and 50s are connecting with fast-growing firms in new industries where experience is in demand. Last year, we also helped many clients in their 60s.

Just for the record, a common thread bound the following people: Commodore Vanderbilt, Socrates, Pasteur, Voltaire, Newton, Talleyrand, Thomas Jefferson, Galileo, Martha Graham, Armand Hammer, Grandma Moses, Adolph Zuckor, Ronald Reagan, Coco Chanel, Dr. Benjamin Spock, Winston Churchill and George Burns. Each made his or her major accomplishments after becoming a "senior citizen." So, don't put any limits on your own thinking!

Supplemental #2

Turning Unemployment
to Your Advantage.

When you are unemployed, your advantage is your time, and your ability to get going on an aggressive scale.

Seven key steps if you become unemployed

As a group, virtually everyone who becomes unemployed, becomes reemployed, but some do it quickly, while others struggle, give up or settle for poor positions. With the right effort many can win new jobs that are more attractive than what they had and in healthy industries.

Experience has shown that as time passes, the less capable you will be (both psychologically and emotionally) to do what must be done to win a new job. So, the key is to have a schedule of full activity: breakfast and lunch meetings, interviews, letter writing, phone calls, follow-ups, and negotiations.

For action oriented people, being unemployed simply means having the time to do a lot of the things that need to be done. In fact, the experience of talking to so many people can be exhilarating. On the other hand, many people, if they aren't active... quickly get discouraged.

1. Get support from your employer. Many employers are concerned about the people they terminate and want to provide as much support as they can.

- With respect to severance, corporations will sometimes extend financial support, or maintain benefits.
- Some firms will extend outplacement assistance.
- You also want to make sure there is total agreement on the reason for your separation. Work out an explanation which puts you in the best possible light.

■ Once you have arranged for the best possible support, be prepared to explain why you are unemployed. You can state that the termination was due to factors beyond anyone's control, such as a cutback, merger, or reorganization.

■ You can point out that the company provided a generous severance to show their appreciation, and to give you time to deal from strength.

■ Where it applies, make the point that the final separation was made at your initiative because you are a loyal person who gives 100% and you did not want to look for a job while drawing a paycheck, or take a lesser position.

■ Be ready to provide references who will speak enthusiastically, not only about your ability to perform, but your character and personality as well. Consider people you worked with, those who worked for you, customers, suppliers, or influential people in any part of the company.

■ Don't make the mistake of implying threats. If you are in a position to harm your employer, they will know about it without your saying so, and they'll take it into account when they deal with you. It is to your advantage that your relationship remain positive.

■ If you are terminated for performance, remind your previous employer that judgments about performance can be subjective, and point out that you could be seriously harmed by a negative reference.

2. Build job hunting knowledge. You need to do this every day until you have a new job.

3. Get yourself a mentor... as a sounding board. It can be anyone you respect. You need to share your progress with that person throughout your campaign.

4. Create your resumes and letters. As outlined in this text, this means several resumes and a variety of letters.

5. Become "innovative." Set aside one hour each morning to make a list of leads, ideas, and potential people to contact. Look for breaking news about any industry or occupation in which you are interested. Make it a rule to select three new people or companies to contact each day.

6. Be active. Devote two hours a day to sending out letters or phone calling based on a specific plan of action, and work to arrange at least one interview or personal meeting.

7. Maintain a winning attitude. Allow at least a half-hour each day for exercise. Positive thoughts come more easily to people who stay physically fit.

If you will follow this simple seven-step approach, you will find that you can be way ahead of most others who go through this experience.

10 common pitfalls when unemployed

■ **Turning down your first offer.** Even if it is not everything you hoped for, if it offers challenge, and growth opportunities, it should be given careful consideration.

■ **Not being skeptical of the first offer.** This is the reverse of the last point. If a position is obviously not right for you, if it presents little challenge, allows limited personal growth, then say "no thank you."

■ **Being unwilling to relocate.** Sometimes it is better to go where new firms and industries are springing up. While it is difficult to leave good friends behind, most people can adjust far better than they realize, and quickly make new friends.

■ **Not accepting introductions.** We've all heard it. "I'm not going to press myself on my friends." The truth is, most people want to help friends. It makes people feel good to know they've done something, however small, to support your efforts.

■ **Feeling sorry for yourself.** It is a normal reaction, but, who is being hurt by these emotions? The answer is that the person being hurt is you.

■ **Holding out for unrealistic income.** Instead of doing this, consider a two step move. Work in a healthy atmosphere and keep your resume in circulation.

■ **Not considering a career change.** If your present occupation or industry is on the decline, get into an area where opportunities are growing, and build a successful career.

■ **Allowing your health to slip.** Attitude and physical fitness go hand in hand. When you are able to plan your time freely, it's actually easier to devote more time to fitness.

■ **Allowing financial pressure to cause inertia.** Financial pressures are often the toughest to withstand. Don't be afraid to borrow, or to take part time or temporary work, rather than succumb to inertia.

■ **Displaying a bad mood.** There are many outlets for stress, including physical fitness. Besides, a bad mood will alienate those trying to help you. Follow our 7 step plan, avoid the 10 common pitfalls, and use the time advantage that being unemployed provides.

Supplemental #3

When Is The Right Time
To Launch Your Search?

Many people concern themselves about the job market. But, what makes national news about the market will have little to do with the reception you have in the marketplace.

For example, surprising as it may seem, in good economies or bad, every year the total number of employed Americans increases. Furthermore, the openings available depend more on turnover than anything else. Here we refer to people who retire or leave, thereby creating a job opening. Turnover in the U.S. (for all jobs) is more than 25% per year.

Another key thing to keep in mind is that people do have certain career situations that can and will get worse. The longer you wait to make a decision, the worse your situation may become.

The longer a person remains on the brink of losing a job, unhappy every day, under stress or unchallenged, the deeper the hole that person may dig for themselves. In short, the more aggravating their family and career situation may become.

If you wait and allow this to happen, the negative impact on your mental outlook can be severe. You will never be able to approach marketing yourself with the right frame of mind.

Then, there are some liabilities that only get worse with time. If you have topped out, or stayed in one industry or one company for a long time, you will get increasingly less marketable. Of course, age clearly gets more challenging with time. Things will only be more serious later on.

You also need to concern yourself with your achievements that may have been significant, but which can lose their impact. As time goes on, the impact of those earlier achievements will become less and less. With senior executives and high achievers, the impact factor is very important.

Many people remain in negative situations too long, and let their marketability decline. Today, you need to grow your marketability with every year of experience.

Supplemental #4

Will The McKenzie Scott
System Work for Everyone?

No. This system is for the vast majority of individuals anywhere who feel they have a record of achievement at professional, managerial or executive levels.

Furthermore, we believe there are no professional job seekers who could not dramatically increase their chances for reaching their goals by making aggressive use of our resources. However, some start out with such a high degree of difficulty, that even with the leverage provided by our resources, they stand a less than average chance for success in today's competitive environment. For example:

- People seeking relocation, but with no budget to travel to a new location for interviews
- People with very narrow geographical requirements in small second-tier markets
- People who are not legal to work in the U.S.
- Those with extreme specialization
- Those with a severe disability that prevents them from interviewing or speaking easily
- Those with poor educational credentials and limited achievements to compensate
- Those with significant age issues and no record of valuable contributions in demand today
- People who are simply not motivated
- And some who face bias because of personality, appearance, language problems, or depression

People in these categories need to consider that while our resources will enhance anyone's chances, their odds for success will still not be favorable in today's competitive climate.

Supplemental #5

Your Destiny Is In Your Hands...
and Depends on Your Motivation

With our unique resources there might be a temptation to think that little effort is required to win an attractive job.

We wish that all our clients could experience that. But through our regular staff follow-up and online tracking system, we closely monitor the activity of every client, and we have statistics that tell us otherwise.

We especially look at how often and how extensively they make use of our Job Market Access Center. What we have found is that to make our system work, clients must use the center aggressively. Of our most successful clients... people who succeeded in a minimum of time... 92% used it extensively. When we looked at the campaigns of clients whose search took longer than expected, we found that most *had not taken aggressive advantage* of our information.

The implications are clear. Similar to any other resources you might purchase to help you achieve a goal, no matter how effective they might have been for thousands of others, they will work for you only if you use them.

Attending the finest golf school will not lower your score unless you practice regularly. The most effective weight loss program works only if you adhere to what it requires. The most rigorous physical conditioning program gets you in great shape only if you get to the gym and do the exercises.

Likewise, if you decide to make use of our extensive resources, it is your responsibility to make the most of them. You will need to access them on a daily basis, take advantage of the ability to quickly find information and contacts others cannot, and be as creative and aggressive as you need to be in order to surface the right opportunities.

Supplemental #6

A Brief Postscript For
McKenzie Scott Clients

We have pioneered a range of resources that previously have never been available. This handbook is your step-by-step guide to using these resources, and to maximizing your market exposure. Here is a sample of our capability.

■ **Marketing game plans.** A staff team can study your situation and identify all your assets and transferable skills to be marketed, pinpoint your best career and industry options and suggest goals. We can also provide ways for neutralizing any liabilities and supply a step-by-step game plan for getting the right interviews. The idea is to reduce trial and error and cut job hunting time by up to 50%.

■ **Professional resume and letter writing.** We can also create compelling materials of distinction... documents which capture the best expression of your talents.

■ **Marketing you thru custom resume distributions and mailings.** We can distribute your resumes to thousands of recruiters, growth firms, medium/large employers and VCs. Done quickly, this can give you an immense advantage.

■ **Job hunting team support.** We can make experts available throughout... to be a sounding board when needed, to help strategize all interviews, supply course corrections, draft all letters you need and assist in negotiations.

■ **You can have unlimited use of our Job Market Access Center.** The result of years of work, and millions invested, this gives you the information you need as you go through your search.

How McKenzie Scott Organizes
to Help Each Client.

We assign a team to market you:

A Marketing Director
A Research / Internet Specialist
A Client Services Specialist

Resume distribution staff, writers and negotiation specialists also participate.

We use team support because we have found that the most successful searches follow a classic business principle. An organized team, with access to the right resources, will invariably outperform the inexperienced individual.

A Brief Overview of What The McKenzie Scott Job Market Access Center Does For You

One of the greatest challenges in any job search is being able to find the right openings and leads. We are helping solve this challenge through our Job Market Access Center. Here's what it provides.

1

Continuous access to the openings you need
We provide access to virtually everything that's important in the published job market... over 1,700,000 openings at any moment in time. You can instantly access openings by location and income level.

2

Continuous access to the leads you need
We supply breaking business news as it occurs, sorted by the location and industries you prefer. These events are often leads to emerging jobs.

3

Market intelligence that can help you
Through our Job Market Access Center, you can also instantly review special reports on companies and industries that may interest you.

4

Continuous research support—that can help you
Our unsurpassed research center can also provide custom information regarding almost anything you need. All you do is email your requests on simple order forms.

5

Online advice and counsel—if needed
As you go through your search, you can also get instant advice... on almost any job hunting subject of interest.

- Openings from 100,000 employers
- Openings from 3,000 newspapers
- Openings from 2,100 trade magazines
- Openings from 300 job boards
- Openings from 3,500 recruiters posting openings on the web

- Firms getting capital... and new startup organizations
- Firms announcing record sales, profits and new contracts
- New CEOs being appointed
- Companies relocating to your area
- Major new products being introduced

- Company and market trend reports
- Investment banker reports on firms and industries
- Background profiles on 800,000 executives
- Trade magazine analysts' reports on firms and industries
- Information on employers before your interviews

- Custom mailing lists of firms and decision makers
- Information on influential alumni to network
- Custom research to meet your needs

- 3-day workshop condensed to 4 hours on 15 audios
- Access to articles on 90 job hunting topics of interest
- Weekly newsletter and strategy updates emailed to you

There is a major difference between how people find jobs with traditional job hunting... vs. with McKenzie Scott's resources

Without our resources people are rarely able to generate activity in all eight segments of the job market. The result is most people are forced to depend far too much on contacts and networking. Our clients get much broader market exposure, and this is reflected in the way that they end up getting their new positions.

How people get jobs with traditional methods

3%	from contacting employers directly
3%	through answering ads or online openings
9%	through agencies or executive recruiters
59%	from existing contacts and direct referrals
23%	from other networking efforts
3%	by miscellaneous means (placing ads, through trade associations, alumni centers, committee searches, computer match, etc.)

How people get jobs with McKenzie Scott

34%	from contacting employers directly by direct mail and by using breaking news to find emerging opportunities, or by getting a job created for you
24%	through answering ads or online openings
23%	through agencies or executive recruiters
9%	from existing contacts and direct referrals
9%	from other networking efforts
1%	by miscellaneous means (placing ads, through trade associations, alumni centers, committee searches, computer match, etc.)

There is also a major difference in "how long" job hunting takes with traditional methods... vs. McKenzie Scott's average clients & aggressive clients

	Traditional	MCKS	Aggress'v
Scientific	12.8 mo's	4.4 mo's	3.4 mo's
General mgmt.	12.7 mo's	4.2 mo's	3.4 mo's
Legal / consulting	10.6 mo's	4.2 mo's	3.3 mo's
Human resources	10.9 mo's	3.9 mo's	3.2 mo's
Accounting / finance	9.9 mo's	3.9 mo's	3.2 mo's
Misc. staff positions	9.9 mo's	3.8 mo's	3.2 mo's
Operations	9.9 mo's	3.5 mo's	3.1 mo's
Office management	9.4 mo's	3.5 mo's	3.0 mo's
Marketing / sales / PR	8.8 mo's	3.5 mo's	2.9 mo's
Engineering & related	7.3 mo's	3.3 mo's	2.9 mo's
Information systems	7.1 mo's	3.1 mo's	2.8 mo's

These statistics are general data. You need to be cautious in assessing your own situation. With our clients, length of campaigns will vary widely with the level of income, their transferable skills and other credentials. People in mainstream fields *(accounting, finance, sales, marketing, operations, etc.)* can expect to move with greater speed than specialists.

In addition, those seeking major industry changes take longer. However, results will vary most with the aggressiveness of people's searches. Listed in the last column are statistics for people who used our suggested marketing plans and who aggressively used our Job Market Access Center. Not covered by this data is perhaps the most important factor... the quality of the position people accept.

158

Few things in life are more
important than finding
the right new job. Here
are some other key factors
that will play a major role
in your ultimate success.

BE CONFIDENT

Confidence is all about positive expectations for good things to happen. It's essential, because it affects your willingness to commit your energy, time and resources in pursuit of your search.

HAVE PASSION & DRIVE

Passion and drive make a difference. It's all about the work ethic we all bring to the table. Bring the same energy to this effort that has made you successful in other endeavors.

BE COMMITTED

Your degree of commitment will be influenced by your goals. So, select goals that mean a lot to you... and the pursuit of them will keep you committed.

INVEST IN YOURSELF

There is no new product... and there is no new business... that can get started without some investment. The same holds true for your personal marketing campaign. Without it, you run the risk of never getting off the ground.

TAKE INITIATIVES

One of the nice things about having access to our resources... is that you can get creative and very easily take many personal marketing actions you've never done before.

EXPECT TO WIN

In the end... with our system and all of our resources at your disposal, it will all come back to confidence. Make succeeding a self-fulfilling prophecy.

WHEN YOUR JOURNEY IS COMPLETE

When you accept your new employment opportunity, we invite you to continue your relationship with McKenzie Scott. If you will share your experiences and suggestions with us, it will help us pioneer new resources in the future.

When you do this, you are invited to join *"The McKenzie Scott Executive Advisory Group,"* and be eligible for the following:

- Access to our Job Market Access Center, upon request, for a future campaign.

- Resume distribution services for a future campaign to 200 each... employers, recruiters, growth companies and VCs, and 3,000 recruiters electronically.

- Access to our Job Market Access Center for a family member in need of a career change.

- Complimentary access to Executive Search Online for 90 days for your new employer's recruiting needs—upon request.

- Access to senior staff for a brainstorming session on advancing in your new situation.

MCKENZIE SCOTT
PERSONAL MARKETING SERVICES

www.mckenziescott.com